Surfing
in
Heaven

Mike Mulkey

Title: Surfing in Heaven
By Mike Mulkey

ISBN: 979-8-9885478-1-5 (paperback)
     979-8-9885478-0-8 (hardcover)
     979-8-9885478-2-2 (e-book)
     979-8-9885478-3-9 (audio book)

Cover picture by Doc Ball
(color redesign by Mark Brown Digital Arts)

Cover design by Jeprey Semacio Castro

Illustrations by Scott Sutton

All mentions of Trader Joe's in this book reflect my personal views and experiences. They are not intended to represent the views or opinions of the company.

Published by

Surfing For Balance, LLC
Mountain View, California

For Marla

CONTENTS

Foreword i

1st Wave – Longboards to Shortboards

- Growing up in southern California as longboards transitioned to shortboards in surfing.

    1. Waxing Up 3

    2. Malibu and the Greatest Generation 6

    3. Crown of the Sea 18

    4. Heaven on Earth... 29

    5. Mexican Miracle 44

    6. Leisure Society 57

2nd Wave – The Sun is Setting

- The legacy Mom and Dad passed on to the grandchildren.

    7. The Spirit of Char.. 69

    8. Lessons for the Grandchildren........................ 75

3rd Wave – Eight Feet, Cold, and Glassy

- Riding the Silicon Valley Express while discovering the best (and coldest) waves of my life.

    9. Riding the Wave in Silicon Valley 87

    10. Circle of Life.. 96

    11. Peace of Mind 106

    12. HODADS... 113

4th Wave – Stoked!

- Excited about my future as I paddle into new territory.

    13. New Beginnings... 121

    14. The 2X4 127

15. Slow Down 133

16. "We don't do email ..." 141

17. Surfing without a Leash 148

5th Wave – Paradise

- God's promise of Heaven and the wonder that awaits us there.

18. Begin with the End in Mind...................................... 157

19. Opening Day in Paradise 163

20. Heaven Can't Wait.. 171

21. Tides of Evidence 182

6th Wave – Rock Dance

- Learning to dance through life.

22. "A Lotta Shit ..." 195

23. Stop and Smell the Roses 198

24. Marathon Faith.. 203

7th Wave – Kicking Out

- Knowing my future is secure in Heaven as I prepare to kick out.

25. The Future Is Secure 215

26. Kicking Out 219

8th Wave – The Perfect Wave

- My imperfect sketch of surfing in Heaven.

27. Surfing in Heaven 227

28. The End of the Story 240

Acknowledgements 252

Appendices

I. Author's Note.. 254

II. About the Author.. 255

III. Circle of Life Quiz 256

IV. Prayer to Receive Jesus Christ as Your Savior.................... 256

V. "Going to Heaven" Booklist 257

Surfing in Heaven Glossary...258

Foreword

I first got to know Mike on a standup paddleboard on the shores of the Sea of Galilee, the very lake Jesus sailed with his disciples, where Jesus walked on water. We were paddling into a breathtaking sunrise over the mountains of the Golan Heights as if walking across the glassy magenta-scored lake. How cool is that?

Mike and I have a mutual love for the ocean. My favorite activity following a full day of work is driving straight to the Santa Cruz harbor, where my standup paddleboard awaits to launch me into the Pacific Ocean. Paddleboarding is my way of relaxing and unwinding after a busy day. Gliding across the expansive ocean among Northern California's quiet inlets and coves satisfies my soul like nothing else.

As a pastor of 35 years and an author of nine books, I love to hear people express their unique faith journey. Mike fits that bill to a tee as he enthusiastically told me his story. I am struck by how he combined his lifelong background as a surfer with his zeal for Heaven into a story of hope for all of us. Heaven became a game-changer that turned Mike's world right-side up; I think it can do the same for you. Mike persuasively argues there might be waves to ride in Heaven when we get there. That caught my attention.

I accept some responsibility for inspiring Mike along this path. A series of sermons I preached at a Mount Hermon Family Camp in 2004 started him along this path. That was 20 years ago.

Those sermons were part of a series I preached on Heaven over several days. In it, we discussed "what I will be like in Heaven." The Bible describes Heaven as a *physical* place with *physical* objects similar to our lives on Earth today (but much better). The Bible also tells us we will be reunited with our *physical* bodies in Heaven and walk the renewed Earth as *physical* beings. Like our life on Earth today, only a *lot* better.

Who is to say we could not be doing a lot of surfing (or standup paddleboarding) when we get there?

Making Everything New

In ancient Israel, the sea, whether the ocean or smaller bodies of water like lakes, was not generally a place of enjoyment for the people. The Israelites were often fearful of the sea. No one seems to go sailing or swimming or partake in any recreation for fun. They went to the sea because they had to. The sea represented their livelihood for trade and food. But they did not go there to enjoy some recreation.

The Bible talks a lot about the seas in violent terms. Almost every time a body of water is mentioned, it's a place of chaos and terror; Noah's flood, the parting of the Red Sea, the storms on the Sea of Galilee with Jesus and the disciples. Job even compares the sea to a monster.

Our lives today are a reflection of this chaos and turbulence we find in the Bible's depiction of the seas. My job as a pastor is to convince people that only God can calm our storms. Psalm 65:7 speaks of God as the *only* one with the power to "still the roaring of the seas, the roaring of their waves…" Mike gets this. The disciples were astonished at Jesus' control over the chaotic nature of water, even more than the other miracles they had seen.

Is the storm raging right now for you? Are you facing so many trials at once that you are unable to balance? When the storm comes, it's tempting to think all is lost. I want to encourage you to read Mike's book.

The world is without end. Heaven awaits us, and it *is* forever. *Surfing in Heaven* provides hope and encouragement for your future. The opportunities for surfing (and standup paddleboarding) just got even better!

René Schlaepfer

Lead Pastor, Twin Lakes Church (Aptos, California)

1st Wave – Longboards to Shortboards

- Growing up in southern California as longboards transitioned to shortboards in surfing.

1. Waxing Up

The best surfer out there is the one having the most fun.
— Phil Edwards (American surfer)

Surfing in Heaven chronicles a significant portion of my life as a surfer in California, spanning from the 1960s to late 2024. This journey is structured into eight distinct sections, or "waves," each capturing a key theme that brought me closer to the dream of riding perfect waves in Heaven. Those eight waves span over 60 years of my life, although not always in a linear path. In the end, I am the surfer who is having the most fun. Come along for the ride.

Waxing Up is all about the preparation phase of that journey. Any experienced surfer will tell you waxing up is critical to a successful session in the water. Just like a gear check for a skier heading up to the slopes (skis, boots, poles, gloves, goggles …), without it, your future is uncertain. This book follows my pilgrimage of learning to properly wax up every day for the perfect ride that I know lies ahead for me in eternity. To live life to the fullest here on Earth, we must ensure we wax up every day as we await our grand entry into Heaven.

Growing up at the beach in southern California in the 1960s was an idyllic environment for a surfer grom (see glossary at the back). Surfing became my identity as life revolved around a passion for finding the perfect wave. Searching for that wave has burned in my soul ever since Bruce Brown's *The Endless Summer* played at the Newport Harbor High School auditorium in 1966. Any surfer will tell you that there is something extraordinary and exhilarating about paddling into a swell created deep in the ocean and riding its natural energy into the shore. I've been doing it most of my life and have yet to lose that stoked feeling with each ride.

Waxing Up

Before paddling into our first wave, we need to wax up. Waxing up is an essential but often-overlooked component of surfing that helps prepare you for the rides ahead. When surfing at Steamer Lane in Santa Cruz on a cold January day (a favorite spot in the winter), waxing up is a strategic time to prepare your board and your body. This process starts by closely reviewing the elements (surf, tide, wind, crowd, and currents) to determine the proper tactics for navigating the paddle out and determining positioning for catching waves. Stretching provides some additional time to warm up my body and rehearse in my mind the waves I want to catch. Selecting the appropriate style of wax (by water temperature) and thoroughly rubbing it onto the top of the surfboard completes the process.

Firmly attaching the leash to my leg, I am ready to carefully navigate the moss-covered cement stairs and launch into the icy cold water as soon as I see a lull in the waves. The success of my surf session will be directly related to how well I have waxed up.

Surfing in the 1960s required a much more involved process to wax up. Longer surfboards needed a *lot* more wax. Before the advent of the surf leash, wax was critical to hanging on to your surfboard. The last thing you wanted was for your board to slip out of your hands and wash into the beach. Parowax (called "paraffin") was the only choice for wax in those days, a far cry from today's sticky surf wax. Paraffin was hard as a rock, so to avoid scraping off the wax already there, you first had to soften it in the sun (or on the engine block of your car). Applying a bar of paraffin required serious elbow grease, being careful to cover the nose (for hanging five), the tail (for cranking bottom turns), and the rails by the nose (for turtle diving big waves as you paddled out).

The next step was to walk the top of the surfboard with bare feet at the shore's edge to get some of the wax onto the bottom of your feet (there were no booties back then) while rubbing in wet sand to rough the surface one final time. An extra bar of paraffin was stashed into your surf trunks, as you had to repeat the process a time or two if you were out for a long surf session – especially if you lost your board to the beach (the ride-in would slicken the wax). Suffice it to say paraffin was better suited for candle-making.

Now that we are waxed up and ready to paddle out, I hope you'll join me on this journey while catching a few waves along the way. And when you do kick out of your final wave, my prayer is that you'll paddle into Heaven, where perfect waves are breaking right now.

Show me, Lord, my life's end and the number of my days; let me know how fleeting my life is.
— Psalm 39:4 (NIV)

2. Malibu and "The Greatest Generation"

I think this is the greatest generation any society has ever produced.
— Tom Brokaw (T.V. journalist and author)

The Greatest Generation, a book by Tom Brokaw, tells the story of American citizens born into the false sense of prosperity of the 1920s, raised through the Great Depression in the 1930s, and sent overseas to fight for global freedom in World War II during the 1940s. They won the war and returned home to a grateful nation that made it possible for more Americans to attend college than any society before. They then married and gave birth in record numbers to my generation, the Baby Boomers.

Both my father, Jack Mulkey, and father-in-law, John D'Zurko, were a part of this select fraternity who made it home from a war that cost an estimated 70-85 million lives [1]. They were humble men united by shared values of duty, honor, and love of country. The last thing they wanted was a pat on the back for saving the world. Yet their commitment to succeed on all fronts despite insurmountable odds is unmatched in American history today. They truly were the greatest generation.

Dad would describe his experience in World War II as not necessarily unique or heroic since everyone else around him was doing it too. He reasoned that the 70–85 million soldiers and civilians who took their stories to the grave were the real heroes. Otherwise, he hardly ever spoke about his experience in the war. Only later in his life did answers to my many questions begin to sneak out. Following is a brief chronology of those three years to help set the background for my journey.

Dad's Navy Days

Imagine writing this letter to your widowed mother about vanishing from home to fight in a world war *before* turning 16 years old:

> Dear Mom:
> I have joined the navy with Todd. I just couldn't turn down an opportunity like this to join with a good friend the same age as I am. We are leaving for San Diego this morning. I know you want

me to make good and this is the only way I will ever do it, don't worry about me I am in the best hands in the world… (see Note 2)

Dad's childhood had hardships beyond the Great Depression. At age 13 (1939), his father died of Amyotrophic Lateral Sclerosis (known then as Lou Gehrig's disease), leaving him to grow up fast as the only man in the household. Three years later, the Japanese attacked Pearl Harbor (December 7, 1941). Like so many Americans at that time, Dad and his best friend enlisted in the US Navy in 1942 (a month shy of his 16th birthday) to fight for global freedom. Both lied about their age and signed each other's enlistment forms (you had to be 17 to join). Amazingly, no ID was required throughout the entire process. As Dad told it, "At that point of the war, the United States was simply throwing bodies at the problem in the Pacific."

Before Dad knew it, his life was dramatically altered in a mind-boggling series of adventures he never could have foreseen. He was first shipped to the US Naval Training Station in San Diego for two weeks of basic training (boot camp). After surviving that, he was sent north to the Naval Air Radio School in Alameda, California, for a month of intensive Morse code training. He then traveled back to San Diego (Naval Air Station North Island) for a week of skeet shooting under the command of Lieutenant Robert Stack, who later starred in the television series *The Untouchables*. Dad told me his shoulder was sore for weeks after that.

Once he had mastered the art of hitting a moving clay target, the Navy sent him back to San Francisco for his official ship assignment as an Aviation Radioman Petty Officer 3rd Class sailor. Suddenly, he was shipbound with 2,000 others on the 488-foot Dutch freighter *Bloemfontein,* cruising out of San Francisco Bay to Noumea, New Caledonia, an island 900 miles off the east coast of Australia. He was below deck seasick for the entire two-week journey.

Flight crews ready to launch off the USS *Saratoga* (Dad is second
from right in the second row)

From Noumea, Dad climbed aboard the monstrous aircraft carrier
USS *Saratoga*, which had by chance been in San Diego harbor at the time
of the Japanese attack on Pearl Harbor. Before he knew what had hit
him, he was flying off the *Saratoga's* deck in a two-man Douglas SBD
Dauntless aircraft on submarine patrol missions while manning the
trigger of a twin 30-caliber machine gun. His initial flight at sea was the
first time he had flown in an airplane. *Ever.*

It is hard to comprehend what went through his head in all this.
Surely, it was a bit of a blur. He had shipmates whose aircraft never found
their way back to the *Saratoga*. [3] At the battle of Rabaul in the Caroline
Islands (covered by *Time* and *Newsweek*), their planes would have just
enough gas to sputter back onto the carrier deck. Ironically, the area
where those battles took place (Truk Lagoon) is now a major tourist
attraction for scuba diving among the many shipwrecks left behind.

At the time the war ended (VJ-Day on August 15, 1945), Dad was
in transit to Adak Island in Alaska, which he suspected was preparation
for an invasion of Japan. They spent a month in Adak before returning
to San Francisco to celebrate the war's end. He received his Honorable
Discharge (C1766958) on November 18, 1945, three years after enlisting
and just after turning 19.

Birth of a Surf Culture at Malibu

As the world recovered from the ravages of World War II, these early trailblazers of surfing at Malibu had an ideal setting for the birth of a craze that would quickly sweep across the globe. Surfrider Beach at Malibu had the ideal weather, a long stretch of fine white sand, and waves as clean and perfectly breaking as one could find along the southern California coast.

Like others so lucky to return home from the horrors of the war, Dad took advantage of the GI Bill to test out of high school and enroll in the local community college while "living high off the hog," as he described it, on $20 per week compensation from the US government. With a guaranteed income and plenty of free time, Dad became one of a select few who set the stage for a surfing revolution in southern California. His life was a dream come true after all the world had been through.

A spirit and camaraderie soon developed among these early surfers, which boiled life down to its most simple elements. Many called this the birth of the *surf culture* in California. It represented a new way of life outside the usual societal boundaries in southern California at that time. Dad never spoke of it that way. They just survived a world war, many in a direct line of fire. They found the freedom they had fought for, and they would make sure they enjoyed it.

There were many characters in this Malibu crowd of pioneer surfers, some of whom became famous through the many movies Hollywood soon produced on surfing. One of Dad's favorites was Bob Simmons, often called "The father of the modern surfboard."

Dad spoke very highly of Simmons and his influence on the sport at that time. In the picture on the cover of this book, Dad is riding a Bob Simmons 10'9" Plywood Foam surfboard (called a "Foam Sandwich"). This surfboard was a significant breakthrough from the Redwood Planks they had been riding, which could weigh over 100 pounds. A replica of this surfboard sold for $40,000 at the Hawaiian Islands Vintage Surf Auction in 2009. Many have credited Simmons with doing more to reconfigure board design in a shorter time than anybody has before or since. Tragically, Simmons's impact on the sport was short-lived as he died while surfing on a stormy afternoon at Windansea Beach (La Jolla) in 1954 at 35 years old.

Charley French (left) and Dad lugging two Simmons concaves up from the beach at Palos Verdes [4]

Another key figure among this crowd was Doc Ball, one of the most influential surfers in the 1930s and recognized as the first dedicated photographer for surfing. Doc built the first waterproof camera housing in 1937, which he undoubtedly used to shoot the cover photo of this book, taken of Dad at Malibu circa 1949 (original below). Dad didn't realize Doc had snapped a photo of him surfing at Malibu that day. As he recounted the story to me, Dad mentioned being at a party at Doc's house when a friend called out, "Hey Mulkey, check this out. Doc has a picture of you in his photo album!"

Dad riding a smooth Malibu face circa 1949 (Photo by Doc Ball)

As a side note, Doc became a Christian because of a near-death experience when he crashed his Ford Woody into a eucalyptus tree. According to surf writer Gary Lynch [5], Doc had a vision following the accident of standing before God and being asked, "Doc, did you read my book?"

Having no excuse, Doc read the Bible cover to cover over the next year as he was recovering. To quote from his obituary on December 5, 2001, at age 94, "Doc caught and rode his last wave into the waiting arms of his beloved Savior, Jesus Christ." [6]

I would argue that it wasn't his *last* wave. He had many more to come in Heaven.

Mom and Dad

My mom (Charlene) entered the Malibu picture soon after the war and quickly caught fire with a suntanned Jack at Surfrider Beach. Like many couples following the war, they fell in love and fled to Las Vegas to get married before Mom's family in Salt Lake City had time to react. Only Mom's parents, Oa and Paul, made it to Las Vegas in time.

Mom had endured her own set of hardships through childhood. Her father passed away three months before she and her twin brother Charles were born. Her two-year-old sister, Norma, was already in hand as their young mother (Oa) took on the responsibility of raising three kids on her own. Fortunately, Oa had the support of a strong Mormon family who came together for her. Somehow, she was able to make ends meet until Oa married her second husband (Paul) eight years later. I remember one of Oa's sisters telling me how she would help nurse the twins when Oa ran out of milk. They did what they had to do.

Then at the age of seven, Mom experienced a severe brain injury when she fell off the top of a slide, landing on her head at the city park. Subsequently, a blood clot on her brain was discovered, which impeded her motor skills and learning ability. Three years later she underwent brain surgery to alleviate the increasing pressure. Complications arose with hemorrhaging after the surgery, leading to Mom losing her motor skills and speech completely. It took a year for her to regain the ability to walk and talk, although there were still words she struggled to articulate. Oa told me only prayer saved her in the end.

My grandma Oa, Uncle Charles (Mom's twin), and my Aunt Norma's son, Bryce (my cousin), each played a pivotal role in my decision to become a Christian later in life. Although I never converted to Mormonism (LDS), God was clearing a path for me with my Mormon relatives in Utah in a way I never imagined. We will get to that in a bit.

Jack carrying his bride (Charlene) over the threshold in Las Vegas in 1952

Growing Up at the Beach

My earliest memories of the beach transport me to the late 1950s when our family frequented Incline Beach in Santa Monica. We lived just up

12

the hill on 22nd Street. While my recollections of those early years are hazy, one thing remains vivid – the freedom and joy found in playing amidst the great expanse of ocean and sand.

The beach, for me, became a place of complete liberation – an open space inviting exploration and recreation in the purest sense. There were very few guidelines, mostly centered around water safety, and many ways to spend your time, unencumbered by the usual rules and restrictions at home. Life became a very simple event, focused on playing in the ocean, warming up and drying off in the sand, and then savoring whatever Mom and Dad put together that day to eat (which wasn't much if Dad was in charge). These early experiences laid the foundation for a lifestyle that would accompany me throughout my life; it was as if I had discovered my home away from home.

As progress would have it, the idyllic environment at Malibu did not last long. The Hollywood movie *Gidget*, along with several other films, brought untold attention to Malibu, and soon thousands flocked to Surfrider Beach to try their hand at the emerging sport of surfing. Dad saw the writing on the wall, so in 1959, our family loaded up our 1948 Plymouth Woodie and moved 55 miles south to the quiet beach-side community of Corona del Mar (CdM). As he would prove later when he fled southern California to Keahou, Hawaii, he had a knack for discovering the next oasis in the desert, and in 1959 CdM was exactly that.

Mom's dreams were realized with two kids, Terry and Mike, and a beach house she adored just four blocks from Big Corona State Beach. The house even featured a shower in the garage allowing the kids to easily rinse off the sand after a day at the beach. Embracing their newfound California lifestyle, Mom and Dad set the stage for a different way of life in CdM, marking a stark departure from her Mormon upbringing in Salt Lake City. Life in CdM was a source of joy and contentment for Mom.

It is hard to imagine a much better setting to grow up in. CdM became ground zero for my childhood until I graduated from Corona del Mar High School in 1973. The beach served as my home base; it was where my friends and I always seemed to end up when we had free time. Despite regular visits from Mormon missionaries to our CdM residence,

Dad staunchly reserved Sundays for surfing, a decision over which Mom had little influence. I'm not sure Dad ever set foot in a church on Sunday.

Coinciding with the surfing industry's shift from longboards to shortboards during this era, the beach lifestyle at Malibu evolved into a mindset that would profoundly influence my perspectives on the balance of work and life in Silicon Valley years later in my career. Growing up in CdM in the 1960s was the launch pad for how the beach and ocean became a part of me. Surfing San Onofre with Dad then became the catalyst that set the foundation into place. These next few chapters are just a taste of what that ethos was all about. Even though I did not have a relationship with God at this point of my life, I am convinced now He was preparing me for my road ahead.

Trust in the Lord with all your heart and lean not on your own understanding.
— Proverbs 3:5 (NIV)

The Douglas SBD Dauntless aircraft which Dad flew off the deck of the USS Saratoga (Pearl Harbor Museum) – Matthew, Mike, Jack

Notes

1. "World War II was the deadliest military conflict in history. An estimated total of 70–85 million people perished, or about 3 percent of the 2.3 billion (est.) people that comprised the global population in 1940."
Wikipedia:
https://en.wikipedia.org/wiki/World_War_II_casualties

2. Unedited letter written by Dad to his mom in 1942 following the Japanese bombing of Pearl Harbor:

Dear Mom:

I have joined the navy with Todd. I just couldn't turn down an opportunity like this to join with a good friend the same age as I am. We are leaving for San Diego this morning. I know you want me to make good and this is the only way I will ever do it, don't worry about me I am in the best hands in the world. I will probably be home in about 21 days because I will be in quarantine for 3 weeks (looks like I'll miss UCLA's opening game with TCU). I will write first chance I get don't worry about me.

PS I am now 17, so anybody that you talk to or asks you I am 17 and you signed for me, this will help very much.

PS You can get Sam to do the work around the house. He's a pretty good gardener and would be glad to work around the house.

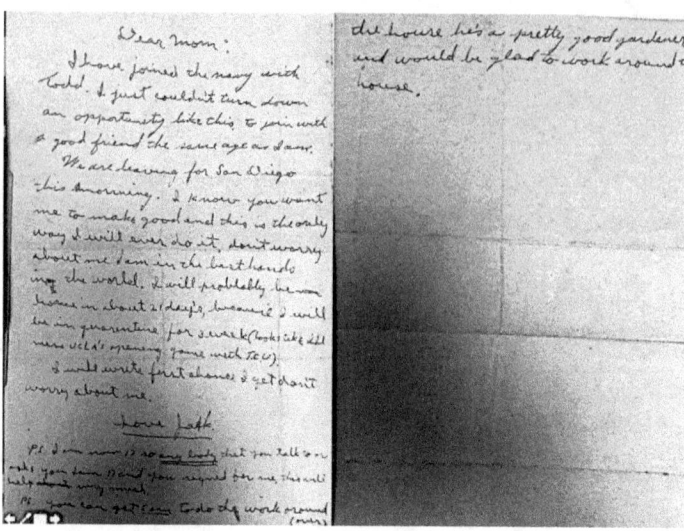

3. Here is an unedited excerpt from a handwritten note Dad sent me describing his experiences:

As I remember I went to radio school for about 1 month, mainly to learn Morse code. Then went to gunnery school for a week on North Island [San Diego] where I shot 1,000 rounds of skeet. Really sore shoulder! That's where my deafness started. When I finally got on the Saratoga & started flying there was a radio silence & no contact was allowed between plane & ship. So much for radio school. I think I flew about every other day. This was for submarine patrol to guard the fleet (at like 4 hours a flight). You just hoped you had a good navigator for a pilot. With no ship to plane contact, and the fact that you were well out of sight of the fleet most of the time, if you missed the fleet on return "that was all she wrote."

When I first got on the Saratoga, we were the only main line carrier afloat. The rest were all in dry dock being repaired. So, we would try to let the Japanese see us and [then] take off, hoping they would think we had more than one carrier available. That was okay with me.

4.   Charley French was Dad's close skiing and surfing friend for many decades. He is still living in Sun Valley, Idaho at the time of this writing, making news as a competitive cross-country skier at 98 years young. As he told me the story of making the two Simmons concave surfboards pictured in this chapter, he and Dad went to General Veneer Manufacturing in LA to purchase the balsa wood, which they then glued together into large planks. They hauled them to Bob Simmons' house and watched him shape them into the concave surfboards. Dad and Charley then took the finished boards home to be glassed and sanded in the backyard, ready for the trip to Palos Verdes.

5.   Gary Lynch, "Legendary Surfers – John Heath 'Doc' Ball (1907-2001)," *Legendary Surfers*, May 29, 2017, https://surfmuseum.org/uncategorized/september-29-the-life-story-of-doc-ball/.

6.   Gary Lynch, "Legendary Surfers – John Heath 'Doc' Ball (1907-2001)," *Legendary Surfers*, May 29, 2017, https://surfmuseum.org/uncategorized/september-29-the-life-story-of-doc-ball/

.

3. Crown of the Sea

Enjoy today ... It won't come back.
— Amish Proverb

Growing up in Corona del Mar (CdM), a quaint beach community in the 1960s, felt like a dream come true. The Spanish translation of CdM, "Crown of the Sea," perfectly captured the essence of our coastal haven. With a population of around 8,000, CdM boasted a small-town atmosphere, stunning sandy beaches, and comfortable southern California weather year-round. From my early days at Harbor View Elementary to our high school graduation at Corona del Mar High School, I shared a tight-knit bond with a gang of friends whose connections endure to this day.

When Dad decided to purchase our home at 507 Marguerite Avenue, just a couple of blocks from the Big Corona State Beach, he understood the rich surfing history of CdM. In the late '20s and early '30s, CdM had been a premier surfing spot, hosting the Pacific Coast Surf Riding Championships (the first notable surfing competition held in the United States). [1] However, a significant change occurred when a large jetty extension was built at the entrance of Newport Harbor in 1936, altering surf conditions and leading many surfers to discover better waves further south at San Onofre. [2]

Despite the shift in surfing popularity, CdM was a gift from Heaven to me. The jetty that once blocked waves became a highlight of my surfing days at Big Corona. When the mighty south swells of summer crashed into it, the resulting rides were unparalleled, creating memories I will cherish for a lifetime.

Reminiscing about my days in CdM evokes the uncomplicated joy of my youth. Beyond the confines of the classroom, we had three main avenues for idling away our time:

1) Engaging in rock-throwing battles in the alley.
2) Playing tackle football or over-the-line baseball at the Community Youth Center.
3) Going to the beach.

Waves or not, most of our leisure time was spent at the beach. As long as we were home in time for dinner, our parents didn't seem to mind *what* we were doing.

While my days at CdM are behind me, the lessons learned there laid the foundation for my adult life. During my time in CdM, God wasn't yet part of my life. Apart from the joy of singing Christmas carols at Harbor View Elementary School, I had no relationship with God. Sundays were for surfing, which suited me perfectly.

This chapter revisits key stories from my CdM upbringing, a life in stark contrast to the frenetic world awaiting me in Silicon Valley's tech industry. It's clear God was guiding my experiences, even then.

The primary charm of CdM was its wonderful beaches. Big Corona, stretching half a mile with pristine white sand, featured a north-end jetty perfect for fishing, surfing, bodysurfing, volleyball, and, of course, girl-watching. It had a snack bar with restrooms and showers, which drew *lots* of tourists in the summer. We labeled the south end "Banzai," which ironically had no shape for surfing at all (due to the jetty). It was where the locals went for plenty of open sand to hang out with friends away from all the tourists.

I fondly remember "corn dogging" in the warm sand at Banzai to heat up your body after a long stint in the water. Once you got too hot, you returned to the water, rinse and repeat until it was time to go home.

On a "red flag" day (meaning, big waves), we would bodysurf Banzai, taking the drop off the lip of the big sets like we were diving off a cliff, getting completely bombed when the entire length of the beach seemed to break at once as your body slammed off the sand bottom. Then quickly swim back out for more.

A short, tubular left wave by the jetty, our impromptu "pipeline," would magically materialize during significant south swells at low tide, providing astonishingly good rides. The moment the lifeguard pulled down the blackball flag, signaling the allowance of surfboards, we eagerly paddled out to savor that elusive barrel.

Little Corona, a more intimate yet scenic alternative, offered minimal sand, rocky coves, tide pools, decent surfing, and no tourists or snack bars. A mile south, The Coves (now Crystal Cove State Park) featured untamed beaches with great surfing and offered freedom from lifeguards to oversee our many escapades, which seemed to materialize anytime the surf was flat. In high school, our small CdM community staged legendary Fourth of July parties at The Coves, which the Newport Beach Police finally put a stop to after our senior year, as they were getting wild. It was a mutually agreed-upon treaty – we pushed their police cars out of the incoming tide while reluctantly agreeing to break up the shindig. Although pictures documenting this event have mysteriously vanished, we can only imagine the relief felt by the Newport Beach Police Department to get out of there without having to call in the tow trucks.

There was also "The Wedge" on the north side of the Newport Harbor entrance, renowned for waves that could top 20 feet on a big south swell. From CdM, we could witness the wave cresting over the jetty on those colossal days, prompting a few of us to swim across the harbor to observe. The covert mission to avoid the vigilant Harbor Patrol boats added an extra layer of excitement, but the spectacle of people bodysurfing those waves just a few feet from the shore made it all worthwhile. Today, the idea of *board* surfing such a wave is commonplace during these imposing south swells, but then, it was unthinkable.

Growing up at the beach in CdM was a lifestyle I dreamed about later in my Silicon Valley career, as I stressed over the many demands in my email inbox.

Foamers

When word got out that a sizable south swell was hitting, Big Corona was *the* place to be. Our tight-knit community of surfers lived for those rare hurricanes off Baja when the CdM jetty would break "off the end." It was all word-of-mouth back then, so the first one to see the swell got on the phone (make that a *rotary dial landline* telephone) and called out the magic words we all lived for:

"It's FOAMING!"

An all-out assault on Big Corona ensued, regardless of what you had planned for the day. Foamers were not something to be missed; they were right up there with Christmas and birthdays. You knew if you missed out you would be hearing about it every day until the next big south swell hit. Someone even graffitied "Pray for Foamers" onto the seawall to remind us about the meaning of life in CdM.

Pandemonium eruption as a set of foamers hits the CdM jetty -
circa the 1970s

When the call hit 507 Marguerite Avenue, I instantly grabbed my Duck Feet fins with a Converse Hodgman raft and sprinted to Big Corona to get in on the action. It was a long paddle/kick out as I slowly passed the massive granite rocks with sharp barnacles that could easily turn you into ground round. Our rafts had no fins and thus zero control, so the thought of "getting sucked" (a term we coined for the dreaded encounter with the rocks) was a thought you had to block out of your mind as you made your way past the seemingly endless towering wall of crusty rocks.

Arriving at the end of the jetty after the long paddle/kick-out, I joined a circle of friends who were fixated on the bell buoy, sitting by itself half a mile further out. It was a crucial gauge for the impending wave size, giving us a 30-second warning before the wave struck the end of the jetty. Everyone's adrenaline skyrocketed when the buoy dipped to the crown, knowing it was a guaranteed massive foamer set. We immediately jockeyed for position, shouting out our claim to the wave of our choice.

"First end!"

"Second end!"

"Third end!"

Pandemonium erupted as the first foamer exploded off the end of the jetty, shooting white water out like the exhaust from a Cape Canaveral rocket launch. Proper positioning was essential as I vice gripped my raft tightly and got as close to the rocks as possible, waiting for the mountain of white water to erupt. The power of that wave coming off the rocks was strong enough to blast me right out of my swim trunks. It was analogous to catching a snow avalanche as it screamed past with incredible speed and force. Once in, the experience was unforgettable — a guaranteed "E-ticket" ride reminiscent of Disneyland's finest. Each of us out there would be talking about those waves for the rest of the summer.

The initial drop was utterly blind. Smothered in white foam, I clung to my raft as if my life depended on it — and it did. It was impossible to gain any sense of where the death-dealing rocks were as I bounced along. The experience was akin to riding a wild bronco in a white-out blizzard or the first ten seconds of skydiving before your static line catches and the chute opens.

Exploding free from the upheaval, I got my first view of the jetty and immediately kicked like mad to steer toward open water to avoid side-slipping out of control toward the massive jetty rocks. We all understood that side-slipping meant getting sucked into the rocks. It was that simple. An incredibly bumpy ride followed, both exhilarating and hair-raising as the gap to the barnacle-crusted rocks quickly narrowed closer to shore. I navigated my raft with precision to make it to the shore break inside, which sometimes earned a hoot from the crowd watching on the beach if you dove into the tube as the wave closed out. It was a very long ride if you made it all the way into the beach (~150 yards from the end of the jetty) that provided plenty of energy for the long paddle and kick back out to do it again.

I vividly remember some of those rides — as if they happened yesterday. Riding that Hodgman raft off the end of the jetty rivals anything I have done on a surfboard since for pure fun and adventure. It was surfing nirvana.

Woody Woodworth (left) and me on a CdM foamer - circa 1971

The inevitable finally occurred when my good friend Mark Magiera, defying the odds, earned instant rock star status (pun intended) by becoming our first hospital casualty while surfing the inside channel of the jetty – where the boats were! Miraculously, he survived the ordeal of getting sucked, setting a record at Hoag Memorial Hospital for the highest number of visitors during his stay.

Mark was sucked into the jaws of the jetty and lived to chronicle his story. We lined up in the hospital waiting room to pay our tributes. In our small community, his story was right up there with receiving the Armed Forces Purple Heart. We were incredibly envious of his bravery and many bandages. Undoubtedly, our parents were astounded by the sudden fame Mark attained for such a daring act.

In response to this ever-present danger, Woody Woodworth and John Park soon pioneered a technique that glued two fins onto the Hodgman raft bottom to enhance wave control. This innovation marked a dramatic shift at Big Corona during foamer days, enabling us to maintain a steady line across the wave without the perpetual threat of sideslipping toward the jetty rocks. A new era had dawned.

John Park went on to found Clear Spirit Surfboards, establishing the first official surfboard manufacturing company in CdM. Johnny began crafting shorter and shorter surfboards for our local crew to test as the new slash-and-thrash generation of surfing started to take hold. When I finally got my Clear Spirit, Johnny and I decided to apply the final "gloss" coat of resin in my mom's bedroom one night after she went out to dinner. We wanted a dust-free environment to achieve a perfectly smooth gloss coat, so we figured what could be better than inside the house? I'm guessing Mom slept well that night.

CdM Shenanigans

If I ever run for elected office (not to worry), our many CdM shenanigans from those days would likely boot me out faster than you can say "Quick Draw McGraw." We were safe and sensible (for the most part), but like any kids, we had our fun and games.

As our surfing improved, we coveted travel beyond the CdM beaches. Sometimes, we could persuade a parent or older sibling to drop us off at a local spot nearby. We had no way of knowing if it would be any good (it usually wasn't), but we always pounced on the opportunity to venture beyond our home turf.

On one occasion, Matt Cox got his mom to drop four of us off at the Huntington Beach cliffs with our boards on a day when there was not much surf. After a very long day on the beach without any food, she forgot to come back to pick us up. Not kidding. Without phones or money, we were shipwrecked. Our young minds were instantly at work on numerous options to save ourselves. Just as we were plotting a robbery on a nearby convenience store to stave off starvation, her car rolled up. We never let Matt hear the end of that one.

If we weren't at the beach, we did have one or two *organized* activities we participated in. Below is an acclaimed picture of our CdM Community Youth Center All-Star baseball team circa 1964. As one can see, we were an elite team of ballplayers, coached by Scott Flanagan's older brother (Scott is in the middle of the top row). The total score of "120 – 0" tells it all. Scott's brother soon learned we had a hard time taking anything too seriously.

CdM Community Youth Center all-star baseball team - circa 1964

I could say a lot about almost everyone in this picture, including the two who opted out of the team uniform (top left). I'll hold it to one person, John "Go-Go" Bandel (top right). Go-Go was a very talented athlete in all sports (especially rock throwing) and simply had a way about him you could not help but like. When we were picking sides, I always wanted to be on Go-Go's team. He was one of *17* children growing up in one of the original (and tiny) two-story CdM homes built in the 1940s. I only went inside their house once or twice, wondering how it worked. It did not seem possible that 19 people could fit in there at the same time, let alone carry on with life.

A funny story about those days was revealed at a CdM wedding reception several years later. One of the Bandel kids was caught in a backyard picking fruit off another family's tree in the CdM neighborhood. When they got caught, they had a piece of paper, which was a detailed map of all the fruit trees in CdM. We confirmed each Bandel kid had an assigned fruit tree to pick for the family on a specific day of the week. Mr. Bandel was one resourceful man.

Once in high school, jobs became a necessity, as our parents (who had survived The Great Depression *and* WWII) held on to the cash tightly. If we needed anything more than a dollar, we had to find a job to earn it. I was a busboy at the Rueben E. Lee restaurant and worked weekends at Ken's Mobile gas station with my friends Danny Moore, Mark Magiera, Frank Frost, and Jeff Zerkie. I realize how important those jobs were to shaping me as a young man. It wasn't like leaving

25

home to fight in a world war, but it did keep me out of trouble (for the most part) and taught me essential lessons in hard work and responsibility with managing money. Of course, we had fun at the same time. Here's one final story to underscore that.

Ken's Mobile was situated in the heart of CdM on Pacific Coast Highway (PCH) directly across the street from Albertson's. Ken seemed to love hiring local CdM high school kids to pump the gas and check under the hood while he was immersed in poker games in his RV, parked in back of the gas station. It was a dream job to get paid to hang out with my best friends, work on our cars, get greasy, and be *the* conduit in town when a big event (aka *party!*) was coming down. It was as if Ken was partnering with our parents to keep us off the streets while simultaneously lining our pockets with a bit of cash.

Weekends were mainly our domain since Ken and his mechanic weren't around much. We had the freedom to run the gas station, and things occasionally spiraled out of control. It was a tad too much liberty for high school boys brimming with ideas.

On one of those weekend days, Jeff Zerkie, Frank Frost, and I were deep into our "Petroleum Exchange Engineer" duties when the infamous "baby's butt" discussion resurfaced. Adjacent to the gas station was a vacant lot sporting a colossal billboard recently adorned with a Pampers ad featuring an overwhelming display of a giant bare baby's butt. It was appalling. We convinced ourselves the entire city was disgraced by it. We even complained to our parents. The situation was an affront that demanded correction, and we harbored fantasies of becoming local heroes if we could do something about it.

The next thing I know, Frank strolled by carrying the extension ladder from the gas station, telling us he had an idea . . . As Jeff and I manned the pumps, we watched Frank climb halfway up the billboard on the ladder and duct tape an M-80 firecracker to the middle of the baby's butt.

"Uh oh . . ."

He then placed a cigarette to its fuse, lighting the other end of the cigarette, and climbed down before the excitement began.

We were all three giggly for what seemed an eternity while serving customers and looking up at the baby's butt with great anticipation. Nothing happened. We concluded the cigarette must have gone out or the M-80 was a dud. Then, suddenly and unexpectedly, it exploded like a cannon on a warship.

KABOOM!

It was ear-piercing, with a quick flash of fire followed by a large plume of smoke, creating a scene we had not envisioned. All cars on Pacific Coast Highway, with screeching brakes, crossed the double yellow divider lines as if "the Russians were coming." [2]

People streamed out of Albertson's across the street to see what happened. We were dumbfounded. We never thought about the impact of such an explosion. Amazingly, no cars collided, and no one was hurt. As we hid in the gas station office, everything quickly returned to normal. Whew. For a week or so after, we were certain every car pulling up with an "E" on the license plate was the FBI coming to interrogate us. But they never showed.

The Pampers ad was replaced a few weeks later. The scar left by the M-80 surely tarnished their brand in a way that needed immediate attention. Mission accomplished.

"I am the Lord your God, who teaches you what is best for you,
who directs you in the way you should go. If only you had paid attention to my
commands, your peace would have been like a river, your well-being like the waves of
the sea.

— Isaiah 48:17–18 (NIV)

Notes

1. Pacific Coast Surf Riding Championships – In 1928, the Corona del Mar Surfboard Club hosted the first notable surfing competition held in the United States at Big Corona State Beach, as it is known today. As soon as the harbor entrance was dredged and over 200,000 tons of rocks were dropped to form the jetty, the competition moved south to San Onofre in 1935 due to the blockage of the surf by the jetty.

2. *The Russians are Coming, The Russians are Coming* was a 1966 American film about the chaos following the grounding of the Soviet submarine off a small New England Island during the Cold War. We were the generation who had nuclear bomb drills in grammar school, where we would get under our desks and put our hands over our heads for protection. The Russians coming during the cold war of the 1960s was not all that far-fetched.

4. Heaven on Earth

I've learned that simple walks with my father around the block on summer nights when I was a child did wonders for me as an adult.
— Andy Rooney (Radio and TV personality)

While Corona del Mar provided an ideal beach community for growing up, my time with Dad at San Onofre most influenced my views on balancing work and life later in my marriage. Just the mention of the words "San Onofre Surfing Club" (SOSC) brings on a rush of heartfelt memories of living an unencumbered life on the beach doing what I enjoyed most: surfing. San Onofre ("SanO" or "Nofre" as the locals called it) was Heaven on Earth to a young aspiring surfer.

SanO holds profound significance for me around a community of families who have shared the waves for almost 75 years along this picturesque, untamed shoreline. This surfing community maintains a camaraderie as strong as the surfers are different. Over the years, the beach has retained its pristine allure, equally enchanting on a brisk winter's day as on a bustling Fourth of July holiday weekend. Dogs, children, and adults of all ages, with plenty of cold drinks and savory food, adorned the beach. On the water, mutual concern for each other thrived among the surfers, with any issues brought forth to an open forum, often in the form of a circle of beach chairs. Access to San Onofre relied on a cooperative relationship with the Marine Corps, bringing together two seemingly disparate groups who existed side by side in a very unexpected way.

SOSC History

The story of how the SOSC was formed is one of the more colorful stories of surfing history. A group of young surfers home from WWII arranging to lease a pristine, secluded surfing beach in southern California from the United States Marine Corps (USMC) for $1 a year seems inconceivable. But that is what happened, and it took a helicopter fly-by 20 years later by the 37th President of the United States, Richard M. Nixon, to overturn it.

With Hollywood surf movies drawing crowds to Malibu, a distinctive surfing haven materialized 90 miles south, near the San Onofre railroad station. The mix of bottom rocks with sand on the seabed produced strikingly consistent waves with a long peeling and gently sloping nature, reminiscent of the waves at the renowned Waikiki Beach in Hawaii. Word quickly spread among the surfing crowd of this gem of a surfing beach called San Onofre.

In the mid-1930s, Lorrin "Whitey" Harrison and Pete Peterson became some of the first regulars at San Onofre, seeking refuge after the new jetties in CdM disrupted the surf there. I had the incredible opportunity to surf alongside them at SanO in the 1960s. Their experiences in Hawaii brought a unique aloha spirit to the beach, perfectly complementing the secluded half-mile stretch of sand backed by dirt cliffs, which preserved an air of exclusivity to SanO. The beach even featured a palm thatch shack on the sand, a remnant from a Hollywood movie company's film shoot.

By the late 1930s, San Onofre had become the place to enjoy the surfer's lifestyle with an unbeatable combination of good fishing, excellent surfing, and a welcoming Hawaiian-style community atmosphere. World War II disrupted all that, changing lives forever. For those lucky enough to return home from the war in late 1945, the USMC began to allow access to the beach again for surfing. The Marines in charge of Camp Pendleton agreed to work out an agreement with these surfers, understanding the sacrifices they had made for our country. [1]

In a remarkable tale of collaboration between civilians and the US military, the SOSC was informally established in 1951, offering a select group of surfers exclusive access to the beach. The SOSC assumed the responsibilities of membership oversight, beach upkeep, and maintaining order, all under a nominal $1-a-year annual lease.[2] My father was fortunate to be among the early members, a privilege my friends and I would soon come to cherish.

This marked the beginning of an era at SanO with roots firmly planted in the simple lifestyle of a surfing society, which soon became a way of life for raising kids at the beach in SoCal. There·were no lifeguards, running water, paved roads, or a way to take a phone call; this was an idyllic world of sun and surf in a serene setting, free of life's pressures and challenges with plenty of time for rest. These traditions would be passed on for generations to come.

In 1969, Richard Nixon became the 37th US president, setting up his summer White House residence near Trestles (a favorite surfing spot just north of SanO) at the La Casa Pacifica. When President Nixon was in town, Trestles was off-limits to everyone, especially surfers. Armed military police would patrol the beach in jeeps, helicopters flew overhead, and an 85-foot Coast Guard ship sat just outside the surf line. Thankfully, the SOSC was just far enough south to be unaffected.

Having President Nixon flying by in his helicopter was a sure sign the tide was about to turn. I will never forget the day in 1971 when I heard the devastating news: the entire SOSC beach had been leased to California as a state park. It appeared to be the end of the SOSC and my dream of passing that SanO baton on to my kids.

President Nixon looked down from his presidential helicopter at the SOSC members on the beach and questioned how they had arranged to gain exclusive access to a US military base. I can imagine how that conversation went. Soon, talks were underway around creating a new California state park, and President Nixon wanted it named after him. In the end, it was deemed a "presidential gift" from Richard M. Nixon – but at least "San Onofre" took the name slot.

Whew.

As has been the history with the SOSC, a few heroes again emerged to keep the club alive and thriving into a new era. One was SOSC President Doug Craig, who provided dedicated leadership and guidance for the club to stay together and work with the state of California to preserve the beach and surfing culture for future generations. The story of President Nixon meeting with the SOSC to gain his personal SOSC membership is documented in the *50th Anniversary Commemorative Album* and is good for a chuckle. [3]

The Waiting Game

My lessons in patience started at an early age with Dad. I waited all week with great anticipation for the weekend trips to SanO with Dad. As good as SanO was for a kid who lived to surf, getting there was another matter – especially considering I couldn't get there without Dad. What should have been a 45-minute drive down PCH turned into a four-hour waiting game for me.

Mostly, Mom did not join us on these weekend journeys to SanO. Our absences were hard on her, as Dad was at work all week, only to take off with me for the beach when the weekend arrived. I would soon find out our weekend trips were taking a toll on their marriage.

Our trip to SanO began with our two surfboards secured with bungee cords on top of Dad's '64 Chevy Nova Wagon driving south from CdM on PCH. The first interlude occurred in Laguna Beach, where Dad would stop to play a couple of sets of tennis with his good friend Jack Upton. I would try to pass the time digging holes, killing bugs, and throwing rocks, constantly hoping it was match point, no matter who was winning (either way, it was "Jack"). After what seemed like an eternity, I knew the match was over when Dad poured ice-cold Tab (the original Diet Coke) into the metal tennis cans over ice. That was my cue to sprint to the car. We were *finally* on our way.

"Aahhhh!" Dad belted out with each thirst-quenching gulp. It was somewhat of a circus act as he juggled the tennis can in one hand, the three-speed column shift in the other, and still managed the steering wheel between them as he pumped the clutch in and out through the maze of Laguna Beach summer traffic and hills. My eyes were glued to the side window for sightings of blue ocean between the buildings, looking for waves as we crawled down PCH, hitting *every* red light along the way. The first marker I looked for was the "Laguna Beach Greeter" (Eiler Larsen) in his bright red coat, who I was sure always recognized me. He gave me a wink and pointed right at me. Next, I watched for a wrecked car overturned on top of a cliff by Poche Beach along PCH. The sighting of the car meant we were almost there.

Our last pit stop off the 5 Freeway was at El Camino Market (Avenida Calafia), where we stocked up on Mug Root Beer, paraffin wax, the LA Times, and a small cluster of grapes for sustenance. Tony Duynstee, the owner of El Camino Market, always greeted us cheerfully at the cash register and provided the latest surf report. It seemed as if Tony was the sole presence running the store. Remarkably, nearly 50 years later, during a SanO trip with my two kids, we pulled off at Avenida Calafia only to find Tony and his El Camino Market still standing. After 75 years at that location, he finally sold the store to a developer.

Strangely, Dad's idea of nutrition often boiled down to little more than grapes and a root beer (after a couple of TaBs in the tennis can on the drive). In hindsight, I realize this probably reflected the challenging times he endured during the Depression and WWII. Perhaps he was also trying to shed some weight; I'm not sure. Reflecting on those days with Dad at SanO, it seems I was learning how to ignore my hunger pains. I recall the tempting aromas of mouth-watering food wafting around me on the beach. Barbecues, in particular, proved troublesome as the smoke consistently blew in my direction. At those moments, having a few extra grapes didn't quite satisfy.

I got my first glimpse of the waves at the renowned surf break Trestles as we exited the 5 Freeway at Basilone Road. My pulse immediately spiked at the sight of those waves; I was giddy with anticipation at the thought of paddling out. Getting the official military salute at the gate to Camp Pendleton was like gaining entrance to Main Street at Disneyland. Those windshield decals that got us by the USMC guard became a source of great pride to signify our status as a SOSC member.

The infamous U.S.M.C. salute to secure passage to San Onofre

We bounced down the rutted dirt road and parked at "Old Man's" to set up base camp: one Coast Hardware beach chair (for Dad), two beach towels, the *LA Times*, and a small Styrofoam ice chest to keep the Mug Root Beer and grapes chilled. Anything coming out of that ice chest needed Dad's approval.

The next hiatus began once we moved the boards off the car to the palm shack. In my younger years, Dad would not let me go in the water until he had been in first. For safety reasons, he wanted to keep an eye on me while I was in the water. Although, every time I looked to see if he saw my ride, he was reading the *LA Times*.

After chatting with friends about the wind, tide, water temp, and LA Dodgers, Dad would finally wax up his board and paddle out. Thankfully, I knew he would not stay in the water long (he never wore a wetsuit), so the clock had now started. Knowing what awaited me was the only thing that carried me over this final hurdle to getting wet – especially if the surf looked good.

"Good grief. . . "

Dad was easy to pick out riding waves as he would drag a foot on his turns, which I now understand was from his days surfing the heavy balsa wood boards at Malibu, where you used your foot as a rudder to turn. My only distraction beyond watching his every move was keeping an eye out for the many bikini-clad women to strut by. Anyone on the beach in those days would surely confirm that Candy McHuen was one of the most eye-catching of them all. Although she was at least five years older, I was sure she noticed me too. Ha.

After what seemed like a scoreless 16-inning Dodgers game, I would race to get my board and wax up as soon as I saw Dad paddling toward shore. The wait was over, and jumping into the water at SanO was the best homecoming ever after that grueling delay. The water washed over me with the familiar smell, taste, and sounds of SanO. This was my home court. It felt right. It was where I was meant to be.

Old Man's is one of the more consistent breaks in southern California, so there were always waves to ride, regardless of the conditions. Once I hit double digits in age, Dad and I could *finally* paddle out together. Surfing with Dad at Old Man's was as good as it got. I knew he always had his eye on me, and I had been trained not to take my eyes off him.

SanO was a unique environment in the water. People looked after each other, paddled loose boards back out (before the leash), and generally cared for anyone in need in the water. It was as if everyone out there was family. An example of this was an accident I had in the surf when I was ten years old. I had wiped out and got walloped in the head by my Dave Sweet surfboard as I fell. That board was like getting hit by a telephone pole, so it opened a good gash next to my left eye with lots of blood flowing. Amazingly, Dad was immediately there and able to carry me like a wounded soldier to shore over the rocks on a low tide day (cutting up his feet badly in the process).

The next thing I knew, I was lying in a van chewing on European black licorice while getting eight stitches next to my left eye ("That licorice is your Novocain," the doc told me). The memory of our hometown doctor praising the quality of the stitching stayed with me. Years later, I learned "Doc" Dorian Paskowitz had performed the good deed. Paskowitz and his family of nine children lived together in a single RV at SanO, seamlessly blending into the SanO scene like fine art. This unconventional lifestyle was par for the course at San Onofre. Paskowitz, a Stanford Medical School graduate, had willingly forsaken his medical career to embrace a Bohemian lifestyle devoted to the sport of surfing.

His unconventional journey was later chronicled in the acclaimed surf movie, *Surfwise* [4]. I recall my dad carrying a bottle of champagne on the subsequent trip down as a token of gratitude for the doctor. That was how things worked at San Onofre – life in harmony. The magic of the SOSC soon got out among the surfing crowd, and membership soared to 1,000 members by 1971 with a waiting list of 2,000 people. Many of my CdM friends were begging me to take them with us. The SOSC had become a mini civilization built around surfing with luaus, horseshoes, surfing and volleyball contests, fishing, Bocce ball, and a Sunday school in the sand for kids. The SOSC was even covered in an October 18, 1965 issue of *Sports Illustrated*, which labeled it "one of the most exclusive and one of the tackiest clubs in the world." [5]

SanO Surfing Contest

Next to Christmas, my birthday, and foamers, the most coveted date on the calendar for me was the annual SOSC surfing contest at the end of summer. Every day I was in the water at SanO, I thought about it, replaying what the announcer (Jim Irwin) would say after a good ride. It was a delightful family event with something for everyone, no matter what your age or skill level. The club members who orchestrated it were the early pioneers of the sport and knew how to run a first-class surfing contest. My goal each year was to make it to the finals, as the trophies were right up there with the Heisman in terms of star power among my surfing community.

For me, it was all about my desire to surf like Erik Hops, who was a competitor in my age group. Erik's father, Frank, was one of the founding fathers of the SOSC. Erik surfed at a level I could only dream about. He won first place nearly every year and was the best surfer I knew. I never saw anyone at SanO with such total board control and ability to walk the nose as smoothly as Erik. He was *famous* in my eyes – my first surfing book (*Modern Surfing* by John Severson, 1964) featured a captivating image of Erik riding a wave at SanO when he was just five years old. To me, it didn't get any better than that. Many years later, when I purchased my first custom Doug Haut surfboard in Santa Cruz, it was a vibrant red pigment replica reminiscent of the board Erik skillfully maneuvered during those early SanO days. To this day, it is my favorite surfboard.

SOSC contest announcer Jim Irwin's voice was appropriately labeled "the Vin Scully of surfing contests." Hearing Jim's booming words from the water made you feel like a world champion, even if you were barely navigating a shore break ankle biter. His enthusiasm was extreme, and his joy of the sport leaped out as he described each ride with fantastic detail and emotion. When announcing the "8-year-old and under" kids, who were barely 25 yards offshore, he made it sound like they were dropping into 25-footers at Waimea Bay:

"The white water is thundering down as he streaks across the massive face of a turbulent curl and cranks a bottom turn just in time."

Hearing Jim narrate the details of each contestant felt akin to perusing a character depiction within a Steinbeck novel. It was surfing poetry at its best, delivered with impeccable voice inflection and modulation that stirred excitement among the crowd, even during lulls between sets. Jim painted vivid descriptions of our rides, creating a connection that transcended mere commentary. The experience was unparalleled, and I hold deep gratitude for this remarkable man. God bless him; I am praying he will announce my rides in Heaven.

The prized SanO trophy with my Dave Sweet in front of 507 Marguerite Ave. (1966)

SanO Today

Taking my wife and children to SanO has been a great joy to see them experience much of what I had growing up. The SOSC leadership has done an amazing job keeping the original structure of the beach intact and maintaining the culture I became so fond of as a kid. We now arrive at 6 a.m. to get in (Dad would not approve.), but once I park the car and collapse into my beach chair, the familiarity of it all comes right back like a favorite song from that era.

I always wanted to experience SanO like the many families who camped there all summer in vans with *lots* of food and drink. We started making an annual trek from our home in northern California to SanO in a fully equipped RV, which allowed us to spend entire days until dark soaking in the San Onofre aroma of a healthy simplicity of life. The kids loved it, and I was thrilled to finally barbecue the meat I always smelled as a child among the many camper vans. We even catch the SOSC surfing contest when we can, which has maintained the same all-inclusive aloha spirit. Jim Irwin has passed on, but his legacy continues from the announcer's booth; those "8-year-old and under" kids are still a personal highlight for me. I tear up every year when I hear it, remembering so well how those words lifted me.

In 2023, I made the trek south for the SOSC surfing contest in combination with my 50th CdM High School reunion that same weekend. The combination of the two was a gift from God. Competing in the "Legends Division" at SanO with Scott French, Bobby Lombard, Tom Beard, and others (Eric Hops has passed on) was a magical experience for me. For starters, we all look exactly like our dads. Ha. We had fun reminiscing the days we competed in the "8-year-old and under" division. It was a picture to me of what we will experience in Heaven – an ageless gathering bound by shared experiences with God's creation. My heartfelt conversations with those men about our early years at SanO have stuck with me. It was a weekend for the ages.

As I contemplate my upbringing at San Onofre and observe my children riding the waves at Old Man's, I bury my toes in the sand, realizing how privileged I am to have experienced such a remarkable environment during my formative years. Sharing this cherished place with my wife and kids brings me immense joy. From the beginning, I believed life at San Onofre epitomized how things should be. Its influence has left an indelible mark on my life.

Fab Four under the grass shack at Old Man's in 2012

I believe a piece of San Onofre will be part of my experience in Heaven. As C.S. Lewis once said, "Aim at Heaven, and you will get Earth thrown in. Aim at Earth, and you will get neither." But at this stage of my story, I was not yet a Christian, so hang on to that thought as I tell you about my Mexican miracle.

My soul finds rest in God alone; my hope comes from him.
— Psalm 62:1 (NIV)

Notes

1.   *The San Onofre Surfing Club, 1952 – 2002: 50th Anniversary Commemorative Album.* This book is a treasure of pictures and stories of the 50-year history of the club. Page 36 describes the new world order at San Onofre following WW II (unedited):

"The Forties – A Changed World"

> World War II profoundly changed America. It ended the Depression, unified, and equalized the country, restarted the economic engine and opened doors to new lifestyles. Those who had never seen the beach till they shipped out of California [from Camp Pendleton] knew they wanted to go back there. Those who had grown up with the beach knew just how good they had it. In 1946 a bunch of us lived down there at 'Nofre: Glen Fisher, Wild Ass Wiley [James] Arness, Bob Card Hammerhead – we'd go to the dump and get old furniture and set it up and live like a hobo camp. We called ourselves the "52-twenty club," cause for the first 52 weeks after the war they paid us $20 a week as veterans. You could live like kings at 'Nofre for that. We all enrolled in college to get better jobs and surfed every day. — Jim 'Burrhead' Drever

2.   *The San Onofre Surfing Club, 1952 – 2002: 50th Anniversary Commemorative Album.* A summary of the struggles between SOSC members and the USMC in the 1950s are neatly summarized on page 41 of this book: "The Fifties – Birth of the Cool." The net of the story is that in 1955 the USMC notified the SOSC they would no longer have exclusive access to the beach. Total chaos followed (unedited):

> Things went downhill almost immediately. Irresponsible surfers set fire to the brush in the San Mateo Creek estuary and nearly burned down the railroad trestle. Burning wood

thrown at the commuter train and piled debris on the tracks once caused a passenger train to grind to an emergency stop. Parking and other regulatory signs were used as firewood. The grass shack was torched. A cave on the cliffs was filled with old tires and gasoline. The fire was so intense the Marines couldn't reach it with the fire truck. Occasionally the MPs were so provoked that they fired rifles and pistols at the trestle surfers. Some surfers set up camp overnight on the beach in defiance of patrolling MPs. The Marine Corps demanded the Club maintain order or all civilians would be restricted from the beach. The Club, of course, disclaimed responsibility since the Marines had allowed free and uncontrolled public use of the area.

3.   *The San Onofre Surfing Club, 1952 – 2002: 50th Anniversary Commemorative Album.* A fitting close to this era is summarized on page 64 (unedited): "Tricky Dick Goes Surfing."

When Richard Nixon moved the "Western White House" to Cotton's Point (north of The Trestle) in '69, 'Nofre was put in the spotlight more than ever. As a result, the Club was now on the verge of being stripped of its beach due to the all-out political battle waged against it. Members had no choice but to play their hands. Bob Mardian (Nixon's Attorney General at that time) was an enthusiastic and active member of the Club and was considered an ace in the hole. Members increased the clean-up detail and suspended members who trespassed on Marine property at Trestles, trying to put on the very best face to the outside world. The SOSC even went so far as to make Nixon an "honorary member" with hopes of wooing his support for a status quo approach to 'Nofre. Tricky Dick was scheduled to meet with them down at the SOSC beach, but, for unknown reasons, he never showed. In 1970, then Club president Doug Craig was permitted a 15-minute meeting with Nixon at the Western White House after Bob Mardian had pulled some strings. Craig believed he had Nixon's backing after their talk. But a year later, Nixon did an about-face and handed San Onofre over to the state as a "Presidential Gift."

The San Onofre Surfing Club's little-known book for members only, published in '74, has a special tribute to Nixon in its closing pages: a picture of Craig standing next to an upright, driftwood log, with a giant middle finger carved into it. "He betrayed us," says Craig

4. *Surfwise* is a 2007 American documentary film about the 11-member Doc Paskowitz family, directed by Doug Pray. The film premiered at the Toronto International Film Festival on 11 September 2007 and had its US premiere on 9 May 2008. Paskowitz went to Stanford University Medical School, became an MD, and espoused a philosophy of holistic health and diet while raising his large family of eight boys and one girl in a camper with his wife Juliette Paskowitz and founding a school of surfing. The film appeared on some critics' top ten lists of the best films of 2008. The film received overwhelmingly positive reviews, holding 98 percent on Rotten Tomatoes. Men's Journal lists it as one of the best surf films of all time – second only to The Endless Summer.
    Source: https://en.wikipedia.org/wiki/Surfwise

5. *San Onofre – Memories of a Legendary Surfing Beach* by David Matuszak is *the* encyclopedia on San Onofre, weighing in at an astounding 1,561 pages and 12 pounds (not kidding). One must see this book to believe it. Page 702 has an excerpt from the *Sports Illustrated* article in 1965, which included the following (unedited):

    At the opposite pole is the San Onofre Surfing Club, which is at the same time one of the most exclusive and one of the tackiest clubs in the world. Founded in 1951 and located at Camp Pendleton, its facilities seem to consist of little more than a few shacks badly in need of repair, which serve as dressing rooms and toilets, and its existence seems to depend on the whim of the Marine commandant. The SOSC has 800 members, each paying $20 annual dues . . . Elderly men wearing straw hats, smoking cigars, and drinking cans of beer sit on the swells astride their boards, occasionally riding a wave in, still seated. One old gentleman says he only surfs on his birthday, of which he has several every summer.

David Matuszak's book can be ordered at: pacificsunset.com

5. Mexican Miracle

Heaven is full of answers to prayer for which no one ever bothered to ask.
— Billy Graham (American evangelist)

To an aspiring grom growing up at the beach in the 1960s, Bruce Brown's epic movie *The Endless Summer* deeply affected me. Brown poetically documented every surfer's ultimate dream on film in an around-the-world quest to find the perfect wave. And find it, they did.

I was 11 years old in 1966 when the movie played at the Newport Harbor High School auditorium. I sat in stunned silence as those around me howled and whistled at the seemingly endless rides at Cape St. Francis in South Africa. Those waves were beyond my wildest dreams. By the time I entered high school in 1969, an obsession with finding perfect waves in Baja, California was brewing. Our many trips south of the border provided excellent surfing on a wholesome diet of Mexican panaderia pastries ($1 a bag), free camping, and 35 cents-a-gallon gasoline. Thanks to our mandatory Spanish class in high school, we became 100 percent fluent in Mexican surf talk with three simple phrases:

- Dónde está la playa? ("Where is the beach?")

- Dónde está el baño? ("Where is the bathroom?")

- Uno más, por favor. ("One more, please.")

Beyond that, not much more conversation was required.

In 1970, I was 15 years old and heading into summer vacation when my CdM surfing bros John Park, Craig Barrett, and Danny Moore came up with a new proposal that was a bit of a twist to our Baja adventures.

"Let's go to Mazatlan!"

The hypothesis was the further we ventured, the higher the probability of encountering those elusive perfect waves we had relentlessly pursued. Our Baja trips were full of adventure and good surfing, taking us 200 or so miles south of CdM. The notion of driving 1,300 miles to Mazatlán seemed like a surefire way to improve our odds, right?

As far as we wanted our parents to know, it was simply "another trip to Mexico." Given that both Baja and Mazatlán are located in Mexico, we deemed any additional clarification unnecessary. In our view, we were merely extending the duration of our stay this time around...

> "Packing for the journey was important. Six pairs of trunks, two boxes of wax, some modern sounds, and in case of injury, one band-aid."
> — *The Endless Summer* [1]

Soon we were stuffing Craig's 1964 bright orange Chevy van with supplies fit for a transcontinental expedition. We had enough canned food for an army, a couple of 8-track tapes for tunes, two beach chairs (doubling as back seats in the van), a tool chest for car repairs, duct tape, water, paraffin wax, a camp stove, and a first aid kit (Band-Aids *and* Tincture Benzoin in case it was serious). To top it off, Johnny was able to sneak two large wooden speakers (from his sister's bedroom) and an 8mm movie camera (also taken without notice from his dad). Four surfboards strapped on top completed the picture of our dream. This mission could be summed up in two words: totally bitchen.

Next stop, Mazatlán.

Or, so we thought.

At age 15, comparisons to my dad joining the U.S. Navy during WWII were surely in order. Bruce Brown's *The Endless Summer* had somehow become my Pearl Harbor. As Craig set the van in motion, I settled into a beach chair in the back, feeling as though I were embarking on an Apollo moon launch. Memories of those SanO trips with Dad flashed through my mind as we navigated south from CdM on PCH.

Our zeal to discover waves in Mazatlán compensated for any lack of experience. Without the convenience of cell phones, the internet, or any means to stay connected with home, we were truly on an authentic surfing safari!

> "Each wave was perfect."
> — *The Endless Summer*

We had not even reached the border before Craig's van hit rough water. We pulled over to a gas station and awaited a diagnosis.

"You're two and a half quarts low on oil."

Ha. Ok. Minor details.

Back on the road with fresh oil and our home speakers booming "Almost Cut My Hair" by Crosby, Stills, Nash & Young (*Déjà vu* album), our next unexpected hazard awaited us at the border crossing in Tecate. We quickly realized how prophetic that song had been as we approached the armed guard at the gate. We could not miss the sign next to the gate guard:

"No Long Hairs Allowed"

That sign will forever be etched in my memory.

Ha – welcome to Mexico.

"Vete a casa, mi amigo." (Go home, my friend.)

The guard's words echoed as he scrutinized our shaggy heads. Our dreams suddenly sank like a WWII battleship under attack by a submarine. Stunned, we turned around and pulled over to the side of the road, engaging in a brainstorming session to explore potential solutions. We assessed the viability of different ideas, including the audacious proposition of having me (with no driver's license) take the wheel and attempt to pass through the gate, given my relatively shorter hair. Fortunately, we conceived a clever alternative: drive two hours east to a different border crossing in Mexicali and try our luck anew.

Taking a more strategic approach in Mexicali, we parked at a gas station just short of the guard gate to doctor up our hair with bobby pins, water, and a lot of finesse. Faced with the prospect of a Mexican barber shop being our only fallback plan, paranoia loomed large as Craig's orange van gradually approached the guard, showcasing our meticulously groomed, all-American appearance. We feigned confidence with our fake smiles as he looked at each of us intently. Miraculously, he signaled his approval for us to drive through. I screamed for joy from my beach chair in the back.

"Dónde está la playa?" we called out as we barreled into the Mexican desert with the sun setting and Carlos Santana singing "Black Magic Woman" (*Santana* album). It was as if we had just won a date with Raquel

Welch on *The Dating Game*. We were giddy in anticipation of the road ahead.

> "It's the kind of wave that makes you talk to yourself."
> — *The Endless Summer*

Just as we were starting to mellow out from our great escape at the border, a third stop was forced upon us. What? A Mexican Federale seemed to drop out of the sky onto the middle of the road as if beaming down from the Starship Enterprise. Feeling snake bitten, Craig heeded his orders to pull over, taking note of the large pistol hanging off his waist.

Encountering checkpoints had become routine during our surf expeditions in Baja, typically involving youthful-looking Federale officers with machine guns. They'd ask a few questions, inspect the glove compartment for marijuana, and then wave us on our way with their machine guns. We knew not to ask any questions. This guy, however, did not fit that profile.

"Vete a casa."

Omitting the customary "friend" from his address, he made it abundantly clear he was not joking about sending us back home. Using just a few words and a stern index finger pointed in emphasis, he conveyed that a "Turista" sticker was required on our car to venture *anywhere* into mainland Mexico from the US. This was news to us. I had not once read about "Turista" stickers in my many issues of the surfer's encyclopedia: *Surfer Magazine*.

In an instant, our endless Mexican summer was coming to an abrupt and painful end. This armed and badged Federale officer was pulling the plug on our Mazatlán wave machine. We were being sent home. It was "adios amigo" time.

We were crushed. I can remember a few tears being shed as we considered the drive back home. This guy was clearly experiencing personal satisfaction in sending four long-haired gringos back to mamá. It seemed there was no way around him; he stood like a monolithic obstruction reminiscent of *2001: A Space Odyssey*, blocking the road ahead. It was hopeless.

As we discussed our dilemma, Johnny suddenly blurted out that we should pray. I thought he was kidding. I didn't go to church *or* read the Bible, so I couldn't understand how a prayer would help anything. Calling on God was a completely foreign thought. Our trip was over. There was no way this guy was going to back down. I was already thinking about what we could do with all the canned food and whether we could stop at a panaderia for a final fix of Mexican pastries before crossing back over the border. As far as I could see, it was the end of the road to Mazatlán.

Yet Johnny did go to church and seemed to know something we didn't about prayer. He suggested we call on God to help us out of this mess. If there was a God, I could not imagine He was aware of our current predicament in the middle of the Mexican desert. That was a new kind of thinking to me.

Although it seemed pretty far-fetched, we were *desperate* and willing to try anything, so the three of us quickly got on board and told Johnny to go ahead and pray. The next thing I knew, we were bowing our heads and praying to God for a miracle to happen. I don't think he prayed the Federale would die or anything. I believe it was something respectable and short, like:

"God, please help us. We want to go to Mazatlán to surf perfect waves…"

We all chimed in "Amen" with Johnny; I did know that part of praying from praying with my Mormon family in Salt Lake before meals. It was a heartwarming exercise between us, but I figured that was the end of it. We were going home.

Then, out of the blue, an idea sprang to life among us: "Maybe we can bribe this guy." We had traveled in Baja enough to understand bribery was often effective with the Mexican Police to get them to overlook a traffic violation or parking ticket. It was a daring thought, but like any surfer searching for perfect waves, we were desperate.

Ignoring the shiny gold badge on this guy's chest and the formidable pistol around his waist, we unanimously decided it was worth a shot. After a heated debate on the appropriate amount, we resolved to go all in and present one of our prized twenty-dollar bills. It made no sense to fool with anything smaller. Craig, the elder statesman of our group (by a month or two), was elected to carry out the courageous mission.

Unease consumed me as we collectively returned to the office to make our cash offer to the Federale. Craig initiated the conversation in broken Spanish while nervously scratching his face with the twenty-dollar bill. The thought crossed my mind: What were we thinking – this is crazy. Yet, to our astonishment, the Federale promptly responded with a radiant smile. Instantly, we recognized our ploy had succeeded; *it was a Mexican miracle!*

20 dollars bought a *lot* of pesos back then. This guy snapped up the bait in a New York second and slapped the Turista decal on our car, waving us on our way like we were part of his family.

"Adios, amigos!"

The drums from "Soul Sacrifice" (*Santana* Album) started rolling as we plunged into the darkening desert sky on the rutted Mexican highway. I leaned back in my beach chair, marveling at what a trip this was going to be.

"Bitchen."

That night, we set up camp in the desert and commenced filming the inaugural scene of our Mexican endless summer movie. Following our pork and beans dinner, it turned into a series of wrestling matches in a cactus patch. We embodied the typical behavior one would anticipate from a group of sixteen-year-olds venturing beyond the familiar confines of Baja.

John's prayer had a lasting effect on me. Regardless of whether God directly responded to it, the lesson stuck with me: in moments of utter despair, we could actually turn to God for help, even when faced with seemingly insurmountable challenges. Almost two decades later, when I sought a connection with Jesus Christ, John Park was the one I reached out to. Having served as best man in each other's weddings, our friendship endured, and to this day, we share a close bond as brothers in Christ.

Finding Jesus

At this point in the story, it behooves me to briefly explain how I became a Christian. It is pivotal to my story and helps to reveal how I got here. The Bible is unambiguous: there is only one path to Heaven, and that is through faith in Jesus Christ. Jesus referred to the path as a narrow road not many people are able to locate:

"But small is the gate and narrow the road that leads to life, and only a few find it" (Matthew 7:14, NIV).

At the age of 33, as I started my technology career at ROLM Corporation in the late 1980s – almost two decades following our Mexican Miracle – I embraced Jesus as my Lord and Savior and embarked on a lifelong journey of Bible study. This decision was motivated by a desire to establish a firm foundation for my future in Heaven. A crucial insight gleaned from my Bible studies is that Heaven is not the *default* destination for my future, a topic we'll delve into shortly.

Since making that decision, I have been on a walk of continual growth and wonder about God's plan for my life. The most meaningful change for me was accepting God's control over my life. Although I fight the urge every day to grab the steering wheel, I am slowly learning how it is ultimately in His hands. Writing this book has played a significant role in shaping that ongoing journey.

I pray every day to follow God's plan for my life. That does not mean life has been smooth sailing since I became a Christian. At times, it has been just the opposite, and my faith *has* wavered. Yet, having God to turn to with full knowledge of my ultimate destiny in Heaven has made all the difference. I wouldn't trade it for anything.

This journey commenced one Sunday morning in 1988 when I spontaneously decided to go to church. It was that simple. There were no lightning bolts or voices from above; I just got up and knew I was going to church that day. God did not make it clear to me why I was going; I just knew the time had come. Looking back, I now understand God's Spirit was leading me, though, in the moment, I had no inkling of what lay ahead; I merely followed my heart.

From my limited experience, I only saw two options for attending church. The first was to join an LDS church, influenced by my grandmother on my mom's side, Oa Cannon, who consistently ensured our attendance at Sunday school during our visits to Salt Lake City (a.k.a. powder ski trips for Dad). My Mormon relatives there served as admirable examples, and this option held some appeal. However, the prospect of abstaining from alcohol and coffee, a strict requirement for LDS church members, gave me pause. While I respected my family's faith and adherence to these standards, I doubted my ability to conform easily. I was having too much fun to consider that.

The second option was to attend church with my Baja surfing bro, John Park. I knew John went to church regularly in Newport Beach, and he still enjoyed beer and coffee. So, I showed up on John's doorstep unannounced one Sunday morning in a suit and tie. That is what they wore in the LDS Church, and I had no reason to think John's church should be any different.

I will never forget Johnny opening the door and bursting into laughter when he saw my formal attire. In Newport Beach, an aloha shirt, shorts, and flip-flops were more appropriate – even for church. I was embarrassed beyond words, yet I managed to pull it together and go anyway.

I'd be lying to say it all fell into place from there. It was quite uncomfortable at first, especially singing songs I did not know (my voice was off-key) and reading Bible verses I had never heard of. It was a very gradual process over several years for me to understand the big picture of what was going on. I was blessed beyond description to have a wonderful church with Godly men and women to lead me by example through it all.

Maybe I am losing some of you who view the Bible as out-of-touch with today's world. I completely understand; I was right there with you. I had zero understanding of what I was in for when I decided to follow Jesus. Yet, I wonder where I would be today had I not taken that first step.

Two years later, God brought Marla into my life. We were soon married and moved to Silicon Valley in 1990 to work at ROLM Corporation headquarters in Santa Clara. Embracing our newfound community, we actively engaged in church and Bible studies at Peninsula

Bible Church in Palo Alto, coinciding with the retirement of the esteemed pastor, Ray Stedman. Marla introduced me to Bible Study Fellowship (BSFinternational.org), which became the key to the deep treasures within the Bible. BSF is a remarkable international Christian fellowship dedicated to interdenominational, structured Bible study. BSF led me on an enthralling path of finding my identity by drawing close to God's Word and His plan for my salvation. I am now part of the BSF leadership team for their children's ministry. The weekly cadence of my BSF lessons carries me through life's many hills and valleys by keeping my focus on God's word. It is a lifesaver.

As I grew in my knowledge of the truths of Scripture, Heaven became a topic of great interest. I could never seem to quench my thirst to learn more about it. Belief in the spectacular wonder of what God has waiting for us was a thunderclap of awakening in my faith. Whenever the word "Heaven" appeared, my interest was aroused.

Although Christians embrace Heaven as an integral aspect of their faith journey, my observation has been discussions about it are not frequent. While it is evident Heaven represents the ultimate destination for all Christians, it often remains a mysterious topic not explored in sermons or Bible studies. For me, God's promise of Heaven was crucial to understanding the Bible, and He placed a deep-rooted desire in my heart to get the word out about this world to come and what living there will be like. As you read on, you will see how the Bible and God's story have deeply influenced every aspect of my life.

Their parents don't know.

At my 40th Corona del Mar High School reunion, a classmate (Paula Schneider) approached me and claimed to remember our trip to Mazatlán in 1970. I was astonished. Her family had been in Mazatlán on vacation when our orange van rolled into town with surfboards on top. Incredibly, she bumped into John Park to hear the story of our three-day trek through the Mexican desert and jungle. After talking to John, her dad pulled her aside to say: "I can't believe their parents allowed them to drive down here?"

And, of course, Paula replied: "Dad, their parents don't know."

"With enough time and enough money, you could spend the rest of your life following the summer around the world."
— *The Endless Summer*

We didn't find the perfect wave, but we had loads of fun and created many good stories searching for waves. The journey was peppered with a few wrong turns, including an accidental encounter with the Sea of Cortez that momentarily led us to believe we had reached the Pacific Ocean ahead of schedule.

Then, we thought the trip was over when the van had a complete mechanical breakdown deep in the Mexican jungle on our second day of driving. A Mexican mechanic was working on it when Danny Moore, who happened to be the tow truck driver at our local CdM gas station (Ken's Mobile), put water in the battery and got it to start.

Ha. Another Mexican miracle.

Next, we encountered carpets of dense locust swarms covering the highway and innumerable "Desviación" (detour) signs that sent us onto never-ending dirt roads better suited for motocross than a van full of canned food and surfboards. It was so bumpy that, at one point, the entire tool chest came crashing down on us in the back of the van, almost knocking me out.

It took us three days to finally arrive at the main beach in Mazatlán for our first surf session. The water was so warm (over 80 degrees) the paraffin wax for our surfboards melted, making foot traction on the board very challenging. Little did we know this was the least of our problems.

In our quest for waves, we settled into a campground in Mazatlán, a town that welcomed us, the gringo long-haired surfers from CdM. Unfortunately, our surfing endeavors proved futile due to our lack of knowledge about tide, swell direction, wind, and surf spots. The running joke on the way home was we shot more video of a girl riding her horse on the beach (suitably named "Betty Big Boobs") than of the four of us surfing.

Amid our struggles, we stumbled upon a secluded beach with good potential for waves and decided to paddle out for some filming. It wasn't quite Cape St. Francis, but we could see waves breaking in the distance. Paddling out at an unfamiliar spot felt eerie. I found myself far offshore, scanning the horizon, when, without warning, a giant bat ray launched into the air, landing with a resounding splash just a few feet away. It startled me to the core. I hastily paddled back to shore as if I were the anchor leg in the SanO paddling race. That kind of stuff did not happen back home. I told the guys I'd be glad to film the rest of the day (keeping an eye out for Betty).

As seasoned travelers, we knew to avoid the local drinking water for fear of the dreaded "Montezuma's Revenge." However, despite our precautions, I fell victim to it after indulging in refreshing popsicles from street vendors in town. As perfect storms go, a hurricane was making its way up the coast of Mexico just as I was discovering I could not stray far from the nearest toilet, which was not easy to find.

"Dónde está el baño" became my mantra.

A final and vivid memory of Mazatlán was my getting up at night in the campground in complete darkness to pay my respects to Montezuma in a torrential downpour with gale-force winds blowing our tent apart. Exiting the tent, I inadvertently stepped on a colossal, spider-like creature with my bare foot, hearing it crack like a twig before it scurried off into the night's black abyss.

Adios mi amigo, I am out of here.

We left for home the next day.

From that point onward, only two memories linger from the trip. The first was the sheer ecstasy of stumbling upon a McDonald's immediately after crossing the US border. A Big Mac and fries never tasted so heavenly, providing a sense of homecoming like no other. The second memory was Johnny revealing the film in the 8mm video camera was ruined – we had neglected to read the instructions on properly removing the film, exposing it all. Our Mexican endless summer movie was lost, and not a single photograph remained to commemorate the experience. But the adventure left an extraordinary impression on me. It was a trip for the ages.

Whether God played a role in our Mexican miracle is known only to Him. Yet, I firmly believe our calls to Him in that Federale's office did not go unheard. Looking back, I see His involvement in our journey far surpassed my comprehension at that moment. Undoubtedly, He safeguarded us in ways beyond our imagination. For example, if something serious happened at home, our parents didn't know where we were or how to reach us. Looking back on that trip now, I have a hard time believing God wasn't shepherding us the entire way. I am sure I will find out in Heaven.

Thank you, God.

> "Special thanks to King Neptune for providing the waves
> in this film."
> — *The Endless Summer*

And he said: Truly I tell you, unless you change and become like little children, you will never enter the kingdom of heaven.
— Matthew 18:3 (NIV)

Note

1. *The Endless Summer* is a 1966 American surf documentary film directed, produced, edited and narrated by Bruce Brown. https://en.wikipedia.org/wiki/The_Endless_Summer

6. Leisure Society

A single rose can be my garden; a single friend, my world.
— Leo Buscaglia (Professor & motivational speaker)

The only time in my life I lived away from the ocean (and surfing) was during my four years in college at the University of Utah (the U) in Salt Lake City. These years (1973-1977) marked a transformative chapter in my life, shaping my career and faith, although I was far from seeing it then. Reflecting upon it now, I recognize the profound impact of those years on my journey. A decade away from embracing Jesus into my life, I sense that God's intervention led me to the U, laying the crucial foundation for my future.

I believe in angels. I had Mormon relatives from my mom's side living in Salt Lake City who brilliantly played the part of my guardian angels over my four years at the U. My family was not involved in the Mormon church (The Church of Jesus Christ of Latter-day Saints or LDS). Still, I knew more about them than most kids. My time with them during our annual trips to Salt Lake City made a big impression on me. Our visits with Grandma Oa and Grandpa Paul on Skyline Drive unfolded like magic for me, where our cousins always showed up to play while Dad took in the powder skiing up Little Cottonwood Canyon (only the ski resort Alta was open back then).

My sister Terry and I heading home from another Salt Lake City ski trip in the Woodie (1958)

Each evening, after all the fun and games, Grandma Oa treated us to one of her magnificently tasty, home-cooked dinners.

Anyone who experienced an Oa Cannon meal quickly discovered she could cook like Michelangelo could carve marble. Every meal she cooked was a savory delight and a stunning work of art. She made everything from scratch and ensured it was piping hot when it hit your dinner plate.

My first year at the U, her meals sent me to Heaven and back. My cousins who lived in Salt Lake often kidded, saying I was so fortunate to be the out-of-towner who got invited over to Grandma Oa's for dinner. And it was true. While living alone the first year, the many invitations I received "to come *home* for a meal" meant the world to me. The care packages of homemade bread, soup, and cookies that Grandma Oa left on my doorstep on Friday nights could seriously bring me to tears. They were my saving grace.

Going to the U was not the popular pick among my SoCal surfing crowd in those days. I was told, "The beer tastes like water (3.2 percent alcohol), and the Mormons are everywhere." I would agree on both counts. We used to joke at our kegger parties you'd get equally drunk if you drank that much Kool-Aid. I think there is some truth to it.

Somehow, I made it through high school without a criminal record and achieved passing grades in most classes. However, in a family where college was uncharted territory, I lacked a clear direction for going forward. Fortunately, my then-girlfriend's mother, Pat Gnadt, played a pivotal role by helping me find available financial aid at various colleges, including the U. Following her guidance, I filled out the necessary applications without any expectations. Admittedly, the allure of Utah's renowned powder skiing, just a short 45-minute drive from campus, was part of my motivation.

One afternoon, my life took a dramatic turn when I received a letter from the US government informing me I was awarded a Basic Educational Opportunity Grant (BEOG) to attend the University of Utah. Enclosed were the details of my award, covering out-of-state tuition and expenses at the U for four years.

I was shocked. For the first time in my life, I had a serious path forward in life beyond the next south swell. I am confident it was a gift from God. It altered the course of my life permanently. I often tell people I wouldn't change a thing if allowed to relive those four years.

I will admit to having a bit of sand between my ears when I arrived to tackle my freshman classes in 1973. The year became a complete wipeout. It was as if I went surfing without a fin on my surfboard. I couldn't seem to make one turn without falling. I didn't know how to do this.

My first problem was I had boldly decided to live *alone* in an apartment off-campus with no car and zero friends. I had gone through a fraternity rush week (at Pat Gnadt's suggestion), but it just didn't feel right to me. I felt like I'd be paying for my social life. My pride would not allow that. Unfortunately, Pat had been right. My self-confidence the first year plummeted from lack of social interaction and too much alone time.

Although I suffered from extreme loneliness, my second problem was I wasn't willing to call out for help. The yearning for the beach, my family, and my CdM bros was something I had not anticipated. Worst of all were the nights spent in an empty apartment, dining alone on a can of chili con carne while watching the LA Dodgers game on an eight-inch black and white TV with fuzzy, rabbit-ears reception. The worst of it was the parties I would hear at the fraternities and sororities just up the street. I had to close all my windows and turn up the volume on the Dodger game to block out the lively chatter and music.

I toughed it out through the winter by skiing a *lot* at Snowbird (hitchhiking up and back). I finally made my first friend in a softball class in the spring quarter. Rick Kirschbaum was a wiry figure with a stocky stature and an animated personality I immediately fell in love with. He was also studying "Commercial Recreation" (my soon-to-be-declared major) and would open a chain of successful running shoe stores (Fleet Foot) following our graduation. That gave us an immediate connection, and he soon drafted me onto his softball team. I will never forget Rick's reaction upon realizing my solitary existence that first year:

"Mike, we've got to get you out to drink some beer and party!"

Amen to that.

Surviving and returning for my sophomore year was another "Mexican miracle." I give a lot of credit to my Mormon relatives for being there for me when I needed it more than I was willing to admit. I know they were praying for me, which I now realize made all the difference. The camaraderie fostered by Rick and those kegger softball games on weekends worked wonders for boosting my confidence. Rick and I still cross paths to this day. He is as faithful a friend as I could have found.

Leisure Society

I learned some hard lessons from this unexpected but necessary time of growth and consequently decided to move on campus for my second year. It was tight on my budget, but I knew I had to make a change. The fin had to go back on the surfboard.

I moved into the Bailiff Hall dormitory with a floor of freshman students, who quickly became an inseparable band of close friends. Best of all, two of them (Mike Nejdl and David Crookall) were avid skiers who were drawn to the U because of Utah's renowned powder skiing.

Nejdl was another surfer from southern California who had an unruly head of curly hair and a massive beard that would make Grizzly Adams envious. Beneath the abundant curls, his athletic build spoke of strength and agility, which confirmed he was the real deal in the water too. His contagious laugh mirrored his easygoing personality.

Crookall was just the opposite. Hailing from New Jersey, he came to the U off the icy ski slopes of the northeast hoping to learn to ski the Utah deep powder. He had been on the ski team in high school and was an imposing figure, standing tall and commanding attention with his muscular and athletic build. But his cascade of long, blond hair and the unexpected touch of softness to his persona naturally attracted the women.

As soon as the first snowflakes fell, we were an inseparable threesome on the hunt for fresh powder. We even adopted a designated call when we found it, "Yo Rineeee!" from the TV show *The Adventures of Rin Tin Tin*, which we had grown up with. With a year of skiing the powder under my belt, Crookall and Nejdl were glad to have me along to provide some added instruction. And best of all, Nejdl had a 1970s

Toyota Landcruiser with 4-wheel drive to get us up Little Cottonwood Canyon no matter how hard it was snowing.

"Yo Rineeee!"

Having barely scraped through my first year with a string of C grades, I started to right the ship in my second year. At this juncture, a revelation struck me, altering my career trajectory toward becoming a tennis club manager, which had always been a dream of mine. Dr. Linn Rockwood, from the Recreation and Leisure Studies Department, presented two compelling charts side by side, capturing my undivided attention. The first chart illustrated the projected growth of the computer, a technological marvel yet to fully unfold over the upcoming decades. The second chart depicted the anticipated surge in leisure time among the baby boomer generation as they aged. Both charts pointed emphatically skyward.

I suddenly realized, "Hey, I'm one of those baby boomers."

The computer was going to replace hours on the job with an abundance of free time. Dr. Rockwood's instruction was explicit: "Plan a career in the recreation and leisure industry, and your future will be bright." Thus, a *leisure society* was born.

"Check. *I'm on it.*"

Dr. Rockwood continued explaining that the transition to computers would result in reduced working hours, extended holidays, and more disposable income to spend on non-essentials. He even predicted the four-day workweek would soon come about as the computers did more and more of our jobs. With leisure time surpassing working hours, he anticipated a transformation where leisure would evolve into a wellspring of values permeating our lives. Eventually, a leisure ethic would take precedence over the work ethic ingrained during the era of industrialism.

It sounded a bit like the Roman Empire, but that was okay with me. I was in the right place at the right time. My next move was to declare myself a "Commercial Recreation" major as I envisioned myself running a tennis club four days a week in southern California where I could don tennis attire to work, engage in tennis matches with the pro during lunch breaks, and lounge by the pool to maintain my suntan. Little did I realize this fantasized utopia would not be the cure-all it seemed at the time. I would soon experience that firsthand.

Community

Those next three years at the U can be summarized with one word: *community*. Without it, my first year was a total bust. I then spent the next three years as a Resident Advisor (RA) in the dorms on campus, landing the job soon after moving into Bailiff Hall. The fraternity of residence hall life combined with the RA leadership development training I received enormously impacted me and my future career. It was a community beyond anything I had ever experienced. Developing relationships among 50 new freshman students each school year during one of the most tumultuous periods in their lives was an invaluable learning experience. It shaped me as a person and demonstrated the true value of community.

With room and board covered as an RA, my BEOG grant now provided spare funds for a ski pass to Snowbird ($5 per day for U students) and some new skis and boots. This script just kept getting better. I would get out of class at noon and have my butt on the GAD 1 chairlift at Snowbird by 1:00 p.m. And that was *without* owning a car.

Snowbird quickly became my new San Onofre. The search for perfect waves was replaced by a relentless pursuit of untouched powder snow with Nejdl and Crookall. "Yo Rineeee!" was ringing through the trees almost every time we were out. The three of us watched the snowfall in the Wasatch mountains like the big wave surfers analyzed the swell buoys at Maverick's. Memories of the Little Cottonwood Canyon gate guard shouting out to us, "4-wheel drive, PULL OUT!" are some of the sweetest memories of my four years at the U. We would scream and yell all the way up to Snowbird in Nejdl's Land Cruiser as we flew up the snow-packed highway in anticipation of the deep powder turns we would soon be making.

My one rose in the community garden at the dorms was Reid Miller. I met Reid in my first RA staff meeting in Bailiff Hall. We were reviewing new resident policies when a shaggy-bearded short guy (like me) with Sonny Bono glasses boisterously interrupted to complain about the toilet paper.

Huh?

He proceeded to compare the toilet paper we had in Bailiff Hall to a piece of wax paper.

"It does nothing but smear things around."

Are you kidding me? I had to know who this guy was bringing up a subject like that in front of the entire RA staff (male *and* female).

Reid and I were soon fast friends and backcountry ski partners. He instantly won me over with his complete honesty and warm affability. He even got me to spend my final two summers in Salt Lake City, exploring the many backcountry options for hiking, backpacking, fishing, and more. Growing up in the small town of Tooele, Utah, Reid possessed unparalleled familiarity with the Wasatch and Uinta mountains. He was smart as a whip, awarded "mining engineering student of the year" at the U, and liked nothing better than to venture off into the mountains with a backpack. I was soon drinking deeply from his vast wisdom of the great outdoors as we adventured into the depths of the wilderness together, winter and summer.

Reid convinced me to take off the downhill skis and venture out in cross-country skis to explore pristine powder skiing without a soul in sight. He even talked me into a cross-country ski snow camping trip in the Teton Mountains, the coldest experience of my life. I swore to never do that again. After a couple of nights of misery, we ended up retreating to a toasty motel room in Jackson, Wyoming, where we cooked our dehydrated food and warmed our nearly frost-bitten hands with endless games of foosball in the bar.

Whether tying a hook onto a fishing line or cranking (and banking) a turn in cross-country skis on a deep powder descent, Reid opened new doors far beyond the tides and jetties of Corona del Mar. By the time I concluded my studies at the U and returned to southern California, Reid had gifted me with an extensive encyclopedia of Utah backcountry wisdom. I am forever indebted to him.

The Power of Prayer

Grandma Oa prayed incessantly for me over my years at the U and beyond. I know this because she told me so and wrote her prayers in letters to me. Mom had three other siblings with large families who lived in Salt Lake, and I have no question they were praying for me too. At the time, I hardly thought about it. I was just living my life.

Looking back over my experiences during those four years at the U, I can see God's presence, even if I was not yet a believer. Surely, I will see in Heaven how those prayers were instrumental in developing a relationship with Jesus Christ later in my life. What a joy that will be.

Since becoming a Christian, prayer has been pivotal in my walk with Jesus. The answered prayers, of course, are wonderful. This book surely is one example of that. Mostly though, it's been my daily dialogue with God, helping me steer through the twists and turns life can throw at you. The God who knows all is an open ear to what I tell Him. He meets me wherever I am. Becoming a Christian did not so much change who I am, as it changed who I wanted to be. Prayer has become the avenue for daily conversation with God about how I get there.

I am trying to make my prayers a two-way conversation with God rather than simply pouring out my needs. I like to pause and listen to what He might be trying to tell *me* through the Holy Spirit. I believe God speaks to those who are prepared in their hearts to hear. More and more, I find this time of *listening* to God has been precious and vital to seeing how He might be at work in my life.

I believe God has a specific plan for each life; we are not accidents. He put us here for a purpose, and prayer is how I have drawn closer to God to better understand my purpose here in this life. Prayer helps me to understand the plan He has in mind for my life. When I get to Heaven, the veil will be lifted, and this all will become very clear.

Prayer has also frustrated me at certain times of my life. The inability to see how God is working in difficult situations I am praying for has been quite perplexing. Our family has struggled with serious health issues that years of prayer have not seemed to help. It is easy to think God is not hearing those prayers. Or maybe He does, but not until we get to Heaven do we see how the pieces to the puzzle fall into place. Nevertheless, maintaining my focus on *God* during prayer, rather than fixating on *the mountain* I'm asking Him to move, continues to challenge me.

Recognizing when God responds to my prayers can also test my faith. So often, I pray in earnest for a particular situation, only to lose sight of it as the busyness of life takes precedence. Years ago, I adopted the practice of documenting my prayer requests in my Bible to maintain awareness of God's actions. I jot down the prayer on a page, and when I see God's intervention, I highlight it in yellow. The experience of tracking God's work has proven to be truly remarkable.

One example of this involves a discipleship group of 12 men I met with weekly for two years to study the Bible. We were led by the pastor of our church, Doug Goins. Each week, Doug made sure we devoted time to praying for each other at the end of our study. With all of us having new families and challenging careers, there was no shortage of things to pray for.

Eight years later, our discipleship group reconvened to pray for someone else. Following our prayers, we took the opportunity to catch up on the intervening eight years since our last group gathering. As each member shared updates on their life, a realization emerged – God had been at work, answering many of our prayers. I could verify these instances as I had documented the prayers in my Bible at the time. The moment was emotionally charged as we reflected on God's steadfast faithfulness, even when we had lost track of our prayers over the years. The gradual fulfillment of those prayers happened in ways we hadn't anticipated. We concluded the night with heartfelt praise for God's incredible faithfulness, a truly uplifting experience.

This next section, "The Sun is Setting," was written to honor Mom and Dad and the legacy they left. Despite many prayers both before and after their passing, nothing could prepare me for the void in my life once they departed. Part of that surely is the realization of *my* mortality. Once your parents go, it becomes quite clear you are next. Yet my feelings around the loss of their physical presence in my life were not something I could have foreseen. Words could not adequately express it other than to say life would never be the same without them. My prayer is they both are there to greet me on the beach when I am surfing in Heaven.

But when you pray, go into your room, close the door and pray to your Father, who is unseen. Then your Father, who sees in secret, will reward you.
— Matthew 6:6 (NIV)

2nd Wave – The Sun is Setting

- The legacy Mom and Dad passed on to the grandchildren.

7. Spirit of Char

The Best Things In Life Are Free.
— Frank Sinatra (American singer)

The first 13 years of my life were a fairytale. My mother, Charlene (everyone called her "Char"), was, for me, the *perfect* mom. Mom was a living example of the power of the soul. Her spirit carries me forward each day. God blessed her with an inner joy that rubbed off on everyone she met. Char was a tremendous life force. There was no "half empty" with Char – her glass was always half *full*.

With Mom and Terry at 507 Marguerite Avenue (1973)

All of my friends loved Char. They treated her like a best friend you could always count on for a bright smile. Our home at 507 Marguerite Avenue became party central in my high school days, largely because of Mom's desire to be in the middle of the action with my friends. She had purchased concert-sized speakers for her home so she could listen to Frank Sinatra as if he was singing in our living room. And he was. Those speakers were a huge hit at our parties, blasting music with a force that could be felt as much as heard. We rocked the roof off of our little CdM beach house with Creedence Clear Water Revival, Led Zeppelin, The Beatles, and many more reverberating through the air. Mom let us drink a *little* beer (haha) and even had my friends' parents over to join the action. She figured it was better we were home rather than out on the streets, which allowed her to join in.

Life was sailing along in smooth seas at 507 Marguerite when one day at age 13, out of the blue, I heard these words from Mom:

"Your dad has asked for a divorce."

I will never forget that day. She had been asking me to sit down for a talk, but I kept avoiding it, half sensing something was up. It wasn't like Mom to ask for a one-on-one with me. Then she caught me one day in the house with a good friend. She sat down and just let it out. I didn't react. I don't remember thinking anything. I felt a large void descend on me, but I had no idea what to say. The first words that finally came out were,

"Will I still be able to go to San Onofre with him?"

I had no way of comprehending the scope of what was happening. San Onofre was all I had to hang on to at that point, so it became my focus, and I stuffed the rest deep inside. It hurt bad, but I couldn't admit it. It seemed ironic Dad had lost his father at 13. I believe he felt I could handle it since he had been dealt a similar card. Their divorce rained down repercussions on my world for years to come. Life would never be the same. I credit much of my survival to Mom and her upbeat attitude. She stayed outwardly cheerful through it all, which helped me immensely. She was the one thing I could count on, even though I acted just the opposite.

Following the divorce, Mom was ill-prepared for life without Jack. For starters, she didn't know how to drive a car. Her father, Paul Cannon, quickly bought her a new bright red (her favorite color) 1972 Dodge Duster and asked me to teach her how. I will never forget the first driving lesson. She got in the driver's seat for the first time and asked me which pedal was the "gas" and which was the "brake." Not kidding. That Duster eventually became well known in CdM for "Char sightings."

Managing her money was another area where she needed help. She had never balanced a checking account or learned to write checks. I can remember writing out quick reference cards for her to use at the grocery store so she could write the check amount. Her plunge into independent living was akin to planning an ascent atop Mount Everest without a trail map. Her achievements were herculean, considering where she had come from.

Despite many nights crying herself to sleep after the divorce, she rose above the calamity and created a loving home base for my sister Terry and me. Our home was full of her wonderful spirit, delicious cooking, and an open door to *all* our friends. I vividly remember our high school parties on Marguerite Avenue with Mom in the center of the action, booming Frank Sinatra songs on her ginormous speakers. Char loved Sinatra like bees on honey. The two were inseparable.

While Dad greatly influenced my surfing and athletic side, Mom was the essence of who I am. Even her twin brother (Charles Lloyd) was like looking in the mirror for me. Their mother (Oa Cannon) had as significant an influence on my life as anyone. I got their DNA. The older I get, the more apparent is the connection between Mom and her family for me.

Mom comes from a serious line of progenitors with Mormon roots, including her great-grandmother, Zina Young, who was a wife (among others) to Brigham Young. I am amazed at what Mom accomplished with all the obstacles she faced. Her twin brother Charles was a high achiever, having run track at BYU and earning his doctorate in education at USC. In comparison, it was hard for Mom to be the underachiever. She had to be closely monitored as she was growing up because of her brain injury. Despite private tutoring and pampering from her mother, Oa, she fell behind in school and had to stay back a grade. Yet she maintained her cheer and was determined to be independent. Everyone admired Char's grit and determination to persevere. Her spirit kept her moving forward.

When she reached 18, she flew from the nest in Salt Lake City to find her freedom. She made off to Sun Valley, Idaho, then the Grand Canyon, and eventually descended upon the beach at Malibu, where she met Dad. There, her spirit caught fire, and soon they were off to Las Vegas to get married. Before she knew it, there were two kids (Terry and Mike) and an idyllic beach home in CdM – it all happened so quickly. She even worked at our elementary school cafeteria in CdM, riding her bicycle with a straw basket to and from work. I remember being embarrassed when she passed the school bus riding her bike to work. For her, it had to be the best life she could have imagined from where she had grown up. She was free as a pelican soaring above the waves at Big Corona State Beach.

On January 3, 2007, Mom passed from bed at her home in Santa Barbara into Heaven. She had been fighting an uphill battle with emphysema after a lifetime of smoking cigarettes. The hospice nurses came in and took outstanding care of her for her final days on Earth. We had a memorial service and spread her ashes into the Pacific Ocean on a very cold January 12th. Her twin brother Charles and his wife Alta came in to help us orchestrate the service. They were again playing the role of guardian angels.

My son Matthew (age 11) and five of my closest friends from CdM paddled her ashes out on surfboards to spread in the ocean at Santa Barbara. It was a remarkable event, capped by a school of dolphins who joined in for the paddle back to shore. That evening, we had a festive dinner at a local restaurant celebrating Char's spirit. Many of our CdM friends and Salt Lake City relatives showed up to pay tribute to her life.

I had no idea of the void I would feel once Mom was gone. She was always accepting and supportive of who I was. I can hardly remember her *ever* criticizing me or telling me not to do something I wanted to do. She provided the loving support a boy could only dream of. Suddenly, that was gone.

I read a poem at Mom's memorial service [1], which I wrote at her bedside in 1997 at Hoag Memorial Hospital in Newport Beach. Mom lived just down the street from Hoag Hospital in a mobile home she had purchased on her own. She was very proud of her trailer as it represented her true independence. She had worked at Hoag Hospital for 17 years as a breakfast chef and was well-known for her cheerful greetings to the doctors, nurses, and healthcare workers in the early mornings.

At the time I wrote the poem, Mom had been stricken with a pulmonary stroke and had to be placed on a respirator. Doctors had given her little chance of surviving and told us she would never live on her own again if she did survive.

She lived another ten years, fully independent, continuing to balance her checkbook, drive her car (with a few dents), do all her cooking and cleaning, and enjoy her four grandchildren right up until the day she passed.

Her spirit is a big part of who I am every day.

Well done, good and faithful servant!
 — Matthew 25:23 (NIV)

Note

1. *The Spirit of Char* poem can be found at:
    www.SurfingForBalance.com/resources

8. Lessons for the Grandchildren

Everything will be okay in the end. If it's not okay, it's not the end.
— John Lennon (The Beatles)

If there ever were a perfect sunset, Dad (a.k.a. "Kona Jack") surely would have seen it over his 27 years at the Keauhou Kona Surf and Racquet Club on the big island of Hawaii. It was a nightly ritual for him to collect with neighbors on the shore's edge to stare down the sun as it dipped into the royal blue Pacific Ocean. As the glazed orange ball reached its final glimmer, all eyes were peeled for a "green flash" at the horizon's edge as a final tribute to the day. With the curtain closing and the skies darkening above, Dad would always have a conclusive comment to abruptly move everyone out of their reverie so he could go about his evening:

"Ah, another day in paradise."

Dad slipped gracefully from this life on the night of a full "Strawberry moon" in 2016 on Father's Day. The "strawberry moon" is the nickname for June's full moon, which coincides with the summer solstice. According to AccuWeather.com, the last time these two phenomena coincided was back in 1967, and it won't happen again until 2062. I would guess it has been even longer since it fell on Father's Day.

Dad passed away just four months shy of his 90th birthday. He had just spent the day with his daughter Terry, and her husband, Bob Hankenson. They went out for his favorite meal of fish and chips with his favorite cocktail, a Rob Roy served "up with a twist." As if that wasn't enough of a grand finale, the next morning we found the crossword puzzle from his neatly folded Honolulu Advertiser of the day before – with every box filled in *correctly*. What?

I was on my bicycle en route to work at Oracle when my sister Terry called. In a flash, the world stopped turning. My life immediately took a monumental turn. I had known it was coming but could not fathom the feelings that quickly surfaced.

Dad was a man's man, and I lucked out by being his boy. Life with Dad just happened. We didn't talk things out. We mostly just hung out doing what guys do together, primarily around sports and exercise. He taught me most of what I know about surfing, skiing, and tennis. I don't mean he instructed me; that was not Dad. He was about being together and doing whatever it was we were doing; not much needed to be said. Later in life, I came to appreciate the deep wisdom Dad imparted to me over the years. I wouldn't trade time with him for anything. He took me to school on how to truly relax and enjoy life. This lesson from him was the one I treasured most.

The Bible is crystal clear on the joy and peace awaiting those who place their faith in Jesus. I don't know if that includes Dad. On my last visit with him, I was able to share my faith and communicate how simple it is to accept Jesus into his heart. That was not an easy conversation for me to have with him. We watched a video together on my laptop to get him thinking about Heaven. He did not say much but appeared receptive to what I was saying. It rests in God's hands.

I often dream about being reunited with Dad in the prime of his life in Heaven. It would be a wondrous homecoming. I imagine, of course, he is going to say,

"Michael, let's go surfing!"

Until then, I hope I can have as much of an influence on people as Dad did on his friends and family. Somehow, Dad seemed to rub off on everyone, including people he appeared to ignore. Everyone who knew Dad would agree he left a mark not soon forgotten.

Dad's legacy to his grandchildren can be summarized into six areas. I like to think of it as passing the baton to Marisa, Matthew, Brennan, and Hayley. These are all quite simple – not anything that would surprise those who knew Dad. But the combination of them is what sets Dad apart. He lived each one of them to the fullest.

"Six lessons for the grandchildren," from Kona Jack

1 – Keep your sense of humor.

This may be the most important of all.

Dad was hysterical with his many dry and humorous comments when you least expected them. He had a fantastic wit and was not afraid to use it with anyone. Most importantly, it didn't wane as he launched into some challenging times in his eighties. Dad was a walking comedy act I appreciate now more than ever.

On my last trip to Kona before he passed, I had come to assist him after he took a serious spill walking down a steep hill from the KTA market with a full bag of groceries (in his flip-flops) He was quite bandaged up head to toe and not moving too well when I arrived. His first comment to me was:

"I've lost my swagger, Michael."

I couldn't have said it any better.

His first request was to drive into town for a haircut at his regular barber. I had been there many times with him. As we approached the barbershop, Dad shuffled slowly in as a customer held the door open and patiently waited for him to get by. The guy was looking at him and his bandages with obvious curiosity and sympathy (along with everyone else) when suddenly, out of nowhere, Dad looked up at him and blurted,

"You should see the OTHER guy."

The man holding the door was pausing to process what the heck Dad was talking about when it hit me as I was taking a seat. I was laughing so hard I almost started to cry. Dad just shuffled up to the barber's chair and sat down as if nothing had happened. The barber knew him well and took it in stride as he began dressing him for his haircut.

Dad was not a letter writer, but he was famous for his notes on stuff he would send you in the mail. Often, they were written on a card or piece of paper he reused. He wasn't one to waste paper. Here's one he wrote across an article he sent me:

"Hey, it's not all wine and roses over here! This can be a very tough life, especially if you're in your late, late eighties. I messed up cutting these articles out of the paper, but I'm sure you'll get the drift. -Dad"

This one was written on a copy of the Santa Monica High School alumni newsletter, which included some photographs of his classmates:

"Mike: I have enclosed 2 Xeroxes from the recent Viking news, which is a quarterly published for SMHS alumni. One is a recent picture of Charlie French, which I thought you would like to see. The other caught my eye because I knew everyone involved from my Malibu days. Dave Rochlen is the founder of Jams, and Peter Cole and Buzzy Trent were famous big wave riders (Buzzy looks like he had a couple of 20 footers break on him)."

And looking at the picture of Buzzy, I had to agree.

2 – Sleep trumps diet.

A key to Dad's long and physically active life was his ability to sleep anywhere at any time. He regularly took two naps a day and never (that I remember) had a hard time getting a full night's sleep. I will never forget one incident on the day Marla and I got married. I went into the bedroom to get the tuxedo on and found him flat on his back, taking a nap. I thought he was kidding at first, but with his hearing aids out, I could hardly wake him up.

Dad's sleep habits also seemed to counterbalance his daily nutritional habits, which were not healthy by any standard. He should have written a book on how to live a long and healthy life while eating and drinking anything you want.

My favorite story was the trip we took back to Kona from Queens Medical Center in Honolulu after his surgery to install a stent in one artery. The surgeon had ordered him on a low-fat, low-sodium diet and told him not to lift anything over ten pounds for two weeks. He repeated the last one three times. We were driving back to Dad's place when he had me stop at one of his favorite restaurants along the way ("Michael, pull over here."). I was not surprised when he ordered a giant schooner of draft beer and a large plate of French fries. Of course, he salted the fries heavily and covered them with ketchup.

Picking my words carefully when I mentioned the schooner probably weighed over ten pounds (deciding to ignore the rest), he looked at me like I had gone mad. I will never forget his gaze as he held the giant glass mug with both hands visibly shaking as he lifted it to his lips. It was as if I had threatened to turn off his oxygen.

And, of course, there was Dad's infamous grocery list. Here's one he gave Marisa one day:

Haagen-Dazs coffee ice cream, Ranch-style Doritos, Eye of the Hawk beer, Laughing Cow cheese, Frosted Flakes, Half 'n Half, Snickers bar.

On a thank you note he sent Terry, he outlined what would likely happen to him if money were no object in Kona:

"Terry, I want you to know that I had a big time blowing away your gift certificate at Drysdale's: 1 beer, 3 Rob Roys, 1 stinger on the rocks, and the shrimp basket. So thanks a lot. I hope I can repay you if you make it over in December."

Surely, he slept better than ever that night.

3 – Keep life simple.

Everyone who knew Dad was envious of how he had simplified his life. He had boiled his world down to the bare essentials. He should have won an environmental achievement award for having the lowest carbon footprint in the state of Hawaii. We all have a lot to learn from him in this area.

Dad's wardrobe: one pair of swim trunks for each day of the week

On the day I took Dad to Los Angeles airport for his move to Kona from Newport Beach, I came to the shocking realization he was serious about simplifying. He told me he had sold everything for the move, including his car. It hit me when he got into my car with a single (small) suitcase for his flight and nothing else.

"Dad, where's your stuff? Did you ship it?"

His quick reply:

"This is it, Michael. I got rid of everything."

And he stayed that way. Dad never succumbed to a life of possessions and complexity. Including never again owning a car. His unit #29 at the Keauhou Surf & Racquet Club perfectly exemplifies that. A couple of $3.99 plastic Wal-Mart chairs around a $4.99 plastic Wal-Mart table was the only furniture he needed. He didn't seem to mind that we all had to stand around to talk with him when we visited. I think he liked knowing you would never stay long if you didn't have somewhere to sit. I tried to buy him a Lazy Boy chair several times to help him get his feet up.

"If I want to lay down, I'll just go out to the pool." he quickly shot back.

Good point.

Dad's fantastic ability to keep life simple and avoid the stress attached to the things we accumulate was genuinely something to be admired. Here's another note he wrote us on the back of his race number for the Keahou 5K run, effectively reusing the race number as a notecard:

> Hi Gang: I picked up my race booty, which consisted of two T-shirts in addition to the race shirt (I may not leave much money, but I'll leave a lot of T-shirts,) a twelve-dollar gift certificate at Drysdale's (that's 3 Rob Roys), and a medallion on a blue ribbon.... The weather has been great. Highs in low 80s; lows in high 60s with afternoon clouds and no vog. The snow bunnies are happy.

And yes, he did leave us lots of T-shirts.

4 – Exercise for life!

One quality that most influenced me was Dad's example of consistent exercise throughout his entire life. This was one of the few areas where he did offer advice as we were growing up. Dad believed exercise was a true fountain of youth, whether it was his tennis, surfing, skiing, or even jumping rope in the living room. And he was living proof it worked.

This note on the back of a reused Christmas card says it all:

Life here goes on! Following is my current schedule:
- Monday: work 9-12:30. Tennis 3-5.
- Tuesday: Bike to the village. Coffee at the Pub. Work out at the club and a run. Bike back to the pool.
- Wednesday: Tennis 2-4.
- Thursday: same as Tuesday
- Friday: same as Monday
- Saturday: same as Tuesday and Thursday
- Sunday: rest it up at pool. Tennis 3-5.

Of course there are variations, but not many. I'm sure
you get the idea.

Love, Jack

5 – Enjoy life.

Never one to miss an ice-cold beer after a round of tennis

Everyone who knew Dad agreed he set the stage for enjoying life.
Whether it was a brilliant Kona sunset, an icy cold beer, or a well-played
football game on TV, he enjoyed it to the fullest and let everyone around
him know. This fun quality of his is one I miss a great deal. Dad never
let work distract him from taking pleasure in life and kept a keen eye on
those who did the same. No question a part of this has propelled me into
the work/life balance coaching arena.

Here's an insightful comment he made about Bob Simmons, a
fellow Malibu surfing pioneer, in a note to me about a recent surf auction
of a Simmons surfboard for $40,000:

> "This is the same board I'm riding in the Malibu photo.
> I'm not sure how many of these Simmons made, but
> don't think it could be more than 5 or so. I can only
> remember seeing one other that was owned by Jim
> Arness. Bob was anything but a grinder when it came to
> making boards and never let work interfere with his
> surfing. There seems to be a lot of money out there for
> old surf collectibles. I may be sitting on a fortune."

Dad was not a complainer. Later in life, when the speed bumps (as he called them) started showing up, he would still find pleasure in the midst of it. Don't get me wrong; he let you know if he didn't like something or if something had not gone well. He never dwelled on it, though, and was soon making light of it after.

When we made a trip back to Queens Medical Center in Honolulu for his bladder cancer surgery, he had to carry a catheter bag with him along the way. I could not believe how he kept his spirits up and maintained a sense of humor about it all. I was cringing at the sight of him carrying the catheter bag when we came to airport security and he (of course) got pulled aside for the complete shakedown treatment by the TSA agents. He kept looking at me with an "are you kidding me" look on his face as they patted him down.

"I need a beer, Michael," was his first comment as he rejoined me. I'll never forget that beer. He took a long draw from the cold, wet mug, and belted out:

"Ahhhh, that's a good one, Michael."

I looked at him and wondered how he possibly could be enjoying a beer right now. Yet he savored it as if it was going to be his last.

6 – It's okay to be sentimental.

The family all knew about Dad's goodbyes. They were painful for those of us trying to leave from a visit with him. I dreaded those goodbyes at the end of every trip, as he always started to cry when it was time to say goodbye. My last trip there was the worst of all. It was as if he knew he would not see me again, yet finally just telling me to leave.

The point I think he would make for the grandkids is not to hold your emotions in, but to let them out. I wish I could be more like that. Here are a couple of his sticky notes as evidence.

This one is regarding a blog I had written about my San Onofre experience with him growing up:

"Mike, this is pretty good. I must confess your re-capitulation of a trip to SanO brought tears to my eyes. I've outgrown my motion sickness, but it doesn't look like I'll ever outgrow my sentimentality, which I inherited from my father."

In the mid-80s, Dad took a three-week solo trip to Australia in which the airline (Qantas) lost his luggage on the flight. We were surprised to find a detailed daily journal he kept from that trip where he periodically lamented the loss and its impact on his emotions. His final entry in the journal:

"Checked with Qantas about my suitcase and no luck. Someone else is wearing my snappy clothes and it pisses me off to no end!"

Have mercy on me, O God, according to your unfailing love; according to your great compassion blot out my transgressions.
— Psalm 51:1 (NIV)

3rd Wave - Eight Feet, Cold, and Glassy

- Riding the Silicon Valley Express while discovering the best (and coldest) waves of my life.

9. Riding the Wave in Silicon Valley

If we are enjoying so much progress, why is everyone so worn out?
— Dr. Richard A. Swenson, M.D. (Best-selling author)

Age with wisdom can be a wonderful thing. I look back now on some of the most difficult experiences in my life and realize how they helped me grow as a person and prepared me for the rock dance ahead. Losing Mom and Dad was as challenging as anything I had faced. It shook my foundation to the core. I do believe God has a plan for all of us and our experiences on this earth are not by accident, good and bad. But for me, the loss of my parents was something I could not have prepared for. It changed everything, altering the order of my life. It was as if my compass had fallen overboard, leaving me unable to find my way home.

I was back in the office a week after Mom passed when a co-worker I barely knew, Rodrick Ang, stopped by to check on me. In Silicon Valley, there's little time for mourning. After my one-week bereavement leave, I was expected to return to work at full speed. Rodrick could tell I was struggling and simply chatted with me to see if he could help. He left me a CD of classical piano music performed by his brother, a doctor and concert pianist in Singapore. He told me how in Singapore, people are given three months to grieve after losing a loved one, with no expectations during the mourning period. That sure sounded good to me (and right). I'm not sure I ever fully took the time to heal until I left the tech industry for good. But that's a story for later.

To get back onto my journey from college, my leap from the classroom at the University of Utah into tennis club management back in southern California was a major transition in my life. The turning point came when I landed the position of general manager at the Covina Hills Racquet Club (CHRC) in southern California. CHRC boasted an impressive array of amenities, including 13 tennis courts, two racquetball courts, a weights/aerobics room, a pro shop, a snack bar, and a 25-meter outdoor pool. I was now overseeing a private tennis club of the "leisure society" elite. CHRC members were investing their free time (and disposable income) under my direction. My professor, Dr. Rockwood, would have been proud. It was textbook.

Or so I thought.

I was immediately overwhelmed by the job. Work/life balance went out the window, even though I *was* wearing tennis clothes and working on my suntan. I supervised a staff of 20 employees and managed two full-time tenants (pro shop and snack bar) who required constant attention. The hotel that owned CHRC (Granada Royale Hometels) expected a tennis club to be as impeccably clean and orderly as walking into a hotel room. Inspections from the hotel management staff were constant and militant in their requirements for absolute spotlessness at the club.

To add to my woes, I soon realized CHRC was in a severe negative cash flow position, with membership growth declining and expenses exceeding income. Then we had a pink eye outbreak in the pool and had to close it down, which threw the members into a tizzy. Disgruntled parents were lined up outside my office, wanting to know when their kids could go back into the pool. After all, it *was* summer. Upon inspecting the pump room to investigate, I found my maintenance man sitting in a chair smoking pot. I didn't have to ask about the connection there.

This part was not in Dr. Rockwood's textbook.

Suddenly, my workdays at CHRC went from opening the doors at 7 am to closing the facility almost every day of the week. To make matters worse, my friends were off work (weeknights, weekends, and holidays) when I was busiest at the club. I dropped off all social calendars and even watched my tennis game disappear. The few times I did sneak out to play tennis, I found I was more focused on the condition of the nets and courts than I was on properly hitting the ball. And with an hour's commute to and from the club in West Covina (from CdM), my time in the water to go surfing completely dried up. Work-life balance was not even a thought; I was just trying to find time to sleep.

My Christmas card in 1983 (never miss an opportunity)

When I hired Barry Friedman as the head tennis pro, the tide began to turn in my favor. Barry, a recent graduate from UCLA, where he played four years of tennis, possessed the ideal makeup for CHRC. A truly admirable self-confidence complemented his warm and amicable personality. CHRC members quickly embraced Barry's style and demeanor as he orchestrated activities that boosted morale and encouraged everyone to participate. Barry assumed leadership of the tennis community at CHRC, allowing me to address day-to-day operational challenges so I could get home at the end of the day and maybe surf a little.

Looking back now, there were two critical lessons I learned at CHRC that would impact my career significantly:

- Relationships matter – big time. In a private club, one bad relationship can destroy you. It took just one letter from a disgruntled member I did not take seriously to nearly cost me my job. I survived that letter but vowed never to allow it to happen again. The squeaky wheel really does need the oil.

- Work-life balance became number one on my list of personal priorities. I discovered it is the gasoline that fuels my engine. Without it, I'm useless. Unfortunately, in this job, achieving that balance was nearly impossible, and I soon felt the impact on my overall well-being. At one point, the hotel acknowledged my extensive commitment to CHRC and generously offered me a room next door, which I gladly accepted. However, this only made matters worse. Being just five minutes away from the latest demand at CHRC tethered me there even more. I learned valuable lessons from this ordeal, recognizing its importance for the future of my career.

ROLM

When Granada Royale Hometels announced their shocking decision to close CHRC two years later, in 1984, I took a leap of faith and joined a new telecommunications firm from Silicon Valley called ROLM (where my sister Terry was working). ROLM hired me as a customer support advisor in their Irvine, California branch sales office to help drive maintenance contract revenue for their telecommunications systems, which were just coming off warranty.

I was a deer in headlights. One day, I had been counting tennis ball cans in the CHRC pro shop (in my tennis clothes), and the next day, I was wearing a suit and tie while attempting to count ports on a printed circuit board inside a ROLM Computer Branch Exchange computer (CBX). Of course, I first had to learn what the heck a "port" was.

In the early 1980s, AT&T had a monopoly with analog telephone service in the US. As the US government mandated the breakup of this monopoly in 1982, companies like ROLM emerged to computerize the telephone and long-distance service for businesses. ROLM, a competitor of AT&T, invested heavily in the technical training of its workforce to get a jump on this new opportunity. It was as if I was sent back to college but was getting paid to do it.

Best of all, I met the love of my life at ROLM; Marla was in a customer support role when we first met at the Irvine sales office. A friendship immediately developed. Marla was smart as a whip (USC graduate), beautiful, fun, easy to talk to, and liked to laugh. When I first announced my interest in her, my co-worker Al Walker snapped back, "Mulkey, she's got legs as long as you are." Despite the height advantage, I knew Marla was the one.

I won the jackpot when we married in Newport Beach in 1991. We soon moved 400 miles north to ROLM's headquarters in Santa Clara, smack in the middle of Silicon Valley. There, we planted our roots, raised two children (Marisa and Matthew), and began to call Mountain View home, leaving behind the warm and sunny beaches of southern California.

Selling a ROLM CBX required a great deal of technical sales support. My timing was perfect to enter a program where I received 12 months of technical training classes to become certified as a ROLM systems engineer. Being on the leading edge of a Silicon Valley company like ROLM was exciting. I was in training classes as much as I was on the job. The era of the computer revolution unfolded as a dream realized, and I often needed to pinch myself to internalize I was actively participating in the heartbeat of a global technological revolution within Silicon Valley. The World Wide Web was about to be built.

I immediately took to ROLM's CEO, Ken Oshman (the "O" in ROLM), and his philosophy of "GPW" (Great Place to Work). Those were not just words of encouragement at ROLM; they were genuinely lived out. What made it even better was the opportunity to balance training classes and field sales calls with activities like tennis, swimming, jacuzzi or steam baths, and more. The surreal aspect was realizing you were still technically at work while strolling by the pool on the way to the tennis courts, witnessing bikini-clad women sunbathing alongside a group of guys enjoying Bruce Springsteen's "Born in the USA" blasting from speakers above a bubbling jacuzzi. The recreational facilities at the ROLM campus were comparable to those at CHRC, even gaining recognition on CBS' *60 Minutes*. It truly was a "great place to work."

Marla and I were both enjoying the excitement of our jobs at ROLM but also realized there was not much leisure time to hang out at the beach like we used to in southern California. Silicon Valley was emerging as the global center of innovation for computer technology, so it seemed reasonable that work became the priority. The computer entered our lives in ways we never anticipated in the 1970s. If I read this wave correctly, Dr. Rockwood's leisure society seemed to be in jeopardy. All anyone did here was work.

The following information explosion happened so quickly nobody had time to study the potential dangers that came with it. Alvin Toffler wrote about this in his book *Future Shock*, which became a classic in the field of futurism. Toffler argued the impending information overload would overwhelm society, leading to a state of "future shock" characterized by our collective inability to manage the onslaught. This condition, he argued, would induce disorientation and stress as people struggled to keep pace with the rapid changes in modern society. The more I saw what was going on in the development labs of Silicon Valley, the more I believed he was on to something. There was a wave coming, and it was *big*. Maybe too big.

Ironically, the AT&T telephone, which we phased out with the sale of a ROLM CBX, was initially just a simple voice communication device. However, it swiftly transformed into the linchpin of a technological revolution in Silicon Valley, fundamentally reshaping nearly every facet of our lives. Apple's unveiling of the iPhone in 2007, a little over two decades later, served as a catalyst, inundating our minds with an overwhelming volume of information – exceeding the capacity for any individual to process in a lifetime. Concurrently, it marked the advent of a 24/7 society, a stark departure from the "leisure society" forecast by Dr. Rockwood in my university classroom. Today, we find ourselves immersed in the "future shock" brought about by that singular product introduction, a topic we'll delve into shortly.

During this time of adjusting to life in northern California, it took me five years to brave the cold water in Santa Cruz to go surfing. I hadn't gone five years without surfing since I was born. Some blame was due to the work culture in Silicon Valley, but mostly, it was my fear of the frigid northern California water. New wetsuit technology from O'Neill finally got me to break the ice (literally) at Steamer Lane ("the lane") in 1996. I quickly realized I had found an escape valve from the Silicon Valley pace, less than an hour from my doorstep in Mountain View. This wave became an awakening for me.

CALIFORNIA CLASSICS
STEAMER LANE

This Woody Woodworth poster hung in my office for many years

The lane on a *big* winter swell is not for the faint of heart or inexperienced surfer. Both the leash and wetsuit were spawned there for good reason. The rock cliffs are gnarly, the currents are strong, and the water is numbing. Even getting into the water can be challenging at high tide. This world-class reef/point break is thick and powerful and can break for several hundred yards into Cowell Beach (on a low tide). Paddling out can test even the best surfers, as the currents are strong, and the waves are often too powerful to duck dive under. It rivals any spot I have surfed in California for thrill and length of the ride. The lane is a serious event when it is going off.

There are four different breaks to navigate (indicators, middlepeak, the slot, and the point). I prefer to sit at middlepeak on big days when it can top triple overhead further outside at the point. However, waiting for a wave can get spooky. Middlepeak can quickly jack up to double overhead out of nowhere and get you diving for abalone faster than a boat anchor. The longer your board, the more difficult that can be. The waves at middlepeak often move sideways as fast as (or faster than) they are moving in, so positioning for the take-off can be pretty tricky and involves a bit of luck.

I caught the biggest wave of my life at middlepeak on a monster northwest winter swell one day with nearly perfect glassy conditions. It was one of those days when you could hear the waves thundering before you even reached the cliff to look. And once I did peer over, an outline of white foam stretched from the outer point all the way into the beach at Cowell's. A heavy smell of salt hung in the air, as if a saltwater fog had rolled in, although the air was clear as a bell.

The sensation of this ride was completely alien. I was sitting far to the side of the impact zone at middlepeak when *the wave* unexpectedly appeared and came at me like a freight train out of a dark tunnel, whistle howling. As I nervously angled toward it, paddling sideways as hard as I could, the ocean suddenly picked me up like a tornado and began taking me with it. It was as if all of Monterey Bay was caught up in this wave and I was just along for the ride. I suddenly realized I was moving with the wave and rapidly dropping in, whether I wanted to or not. The wave had caught *me*.

I quickly got to my feet in a crouched position as I raced down the face, noticing a couple of surfers diving for the bottom off to my side and hearing a couple of howls somewhere off in the distance. The drop was sensational, akin to jumping off a cliff. As I started a sweeping right turn, the enormity of the wave and the amount of water moving with me was exhilarating. I felt like Franz Klammer at the 1976 Olympics, racing with abandon to stay ahead of the crashing lip, ignoring all sense of form. I had never gone so fast.

Over my shoulder, I could see the wave breaking behind me in apparent slow motion. Surfers sneaking over the lip looked back down at me as I excitedly banked off the face with water spraying high into the crisp Santa Cruz air like a snowboarder coming off a half-pipe lip. The amplification of the thundering lip behind me kept me racing forward to stay out of danger. The thought of a wipeout here was unthinkable.

My Doug Haut surfboard tracked the face of the wave as if it were the Santa Cruz Boardwalk roller coaster, dropping and climbing as the face continued to build in front of me without any sign of letting up. Each time I turned off the lip of the wave a loud splash of water reverberated into the air. The brute force of this wave allowed me to sweep further out of the section without any danger of losing momentum as I drew out a large arc of a cutback into the power section of the wave. I was flying!

The sweeping turns up and down the steep face continued as the wave refused to relent. I finally kicked out at Cowell Beach a couple hundred yards from where I started as the wave finally closed out in front of me. Cresting over the thick lip, I fell off the back of my board and floated on my back to soak in the memory of what had just happened. I released a light laugh and slowly climbed on my board to commence the paddle back out, reliving every part of that wave along the way. I was giddy from that ride. Like one good shot on a round of golf, it carried me for many, many waves after. It had been a gift from God.

Crossing the chasm into the frigid waters of Northern California to discover there were epic waves less than an hour from home made a world of difference for me in our relocation to Silicon Valley. "Eight feet, cold and glassy" became my mantra. Silicon Valley was proving itself to be the land of endless opportunities. I could get used to this. Even though I had to jump onto an express train every day to keep pace with those around me, I stayed focused on prioritizing work-life balance and not letting my weekends and evenings steal time from my young family. I had learned the consequences of too much work the hard way at CHRC and did not want to go there again.

I thought I was doing a pretty good job of keeping it all in check until my wife delivered a wakeup call one day.

Teach me your way, O Lord; lead me in a straight path.
    — Psalm 27:11 (NIV)

10. Circle of Life

Next to love, balance is the most important thing.
— John Wooden (Head Basketball Coach, UCLA)

Anyone who has known me throughout my professional business career would confirm my claim that balance in life has been my modus operandi. It is in my DNA. As I came into Silicon Valley, aspiring to achieve success and to support our family, I was constantly battling for equilibrium between my work, family, and personal life. Balance became my calling. I launched my website (surfingforbalance.com) in 2014 with that very theme as my mission. I wanted to share my struggles to keep it all in check in this valley of endless opportunity. This book, in essence, narrates the invaluable lessons I learned in the pursuit of balance over my 25-year career journey.

This balance mantra first appeared on my radar screen in a Golden Gate University classroom in Los Angeles one night in 1990. It was an epiphany that stuck. At the time, I was in a master's degree program (Telecommunications Management) to further my education at Siemens' expense. Siemens acquired ROLM in 1989 and I remained with the company as a product manager. Sipping a watery hot chocolate to try and perk up my senses after a long day in the office, my eyes caught the instructor as he entered the room with a folder full of papers in his arms. A bearded man, appearing to be in his forties or fifties, he seemed to be on a mission, exuding a confident and upright demeanor. It was the first day of class, and he immediately handed out what I thought to be a class syllabus. Upon closer inspection, I saw that it was titled the "Circle of Life."

I set my hot chocolate down. This guy suddenly had my full attention.

He opened with this statement.

"I would like to discuss life beyond telecommunications. Where is your life going, and is it where you want it to go?"

Huh?

I reviewed the handout to ensure I had not entered the wrong class. It was, after all, the first day of class. He quoted a Chinese proverb: "If we don't change the direction we are going, we are likely to end up where we are headed."

I could see he was quite serious about all this. He made perfect sense and clearly wanted to deliver his message before we got distracted by the class materials.

He finished with this statement.

"If you can keep your life in balance, you will inevitably be a much happier and healthier person."

His words were simple, yet I knew they were true. This Circle of Life document he had handed out included a self-analysis quiz to help us understand how our life was going. This guy was demonstrating a sincere desire to help us improve our lives at work, at home, and with our personal needs. I could feel he believed what he was saying. After providing 15 minutes of class time to take the Circle of Life quiz, a short lesson followed on how to set goals for improvement in the areas where we had low scores.

The instructor made an eye-opening statement. "A man without goals has been compared to a ship without a rudder. Both are subject to the winds of fate."

At once, I realized I was sailing on that ship. I had a general idea of what I wanted to do in life but could now clearly see no way to measure those desires against the other vital areas of my life. I was simply going wherever the wind decided to take me. It was exciting to put my rudder into the water. Brilliant, in fact. I could now see where I wanted to go and measure the tradeoffs for getting there.

I want to say my life changed at that moment as I reviewed the results of my Circle of Life quiz. Not so. While it prompted me to consider the areas where I wanted to achieve better balance, my life was bustling with a new job, night school for my master's degree, and my commitment to staying in shape for triathlons, leaving little room for anything additional. The handout from the class went into my telecommunications binder, along with the rest of my materials. I did not retrieve it until several years later. A marriage, two kids, and two jobs later.

Ironman Hawaii

The Circle of Life resurfaced when I was working for Sun Microsystems in 1999. My Golden Gate University telecommunications degree had paid off as I landed a Marketing Manager position with Sun's new and emerging "Netra" division. Sun was riding high on the dot-com bubble brought about by the explosive growth of internet-related companies in Silicon Valley. Sun's servers were being marketed as the dot in dot-com. We couldn't build them fast enough.

Sun CEO Scott McNealy had extended a $1 billion credit line to Senior VP Neil Knox to build a family of telecommunications-grade servers for large telecom providers worldwide. The Netra server family was just coming out of development, and Neil needed an accomplished go-to-market team to get the word out to the telecom providers worldwide. It was as if we were pouring fresh cement for the foundation of the World Wide Web. The telco-grade Sun Netra servers were selling like crazy. A constant line of customers waited.

As McNealy himself liked to say when he would periodically address us at our regular beer bashes, it was all about kicking butt and having fun. I could relate to that; bring it on.

Amid the chaos, Marla was learning to manage our home with two busy toddlers as I jet-setted around the world to get our Sun sales teams onboard about the opportunity with Netra servers. Flying to Europe, Asia, Australia, South America, and more, it was an exciting time to be helping to construct the World Wide Web. My leap of faith from the leisure society to Silicon Valley was riding high like the winter swells at Steamer Lane.

Then, a letter arrived from the US mail with the opening line of, "Congratulations!"

I won the lottery.

Well, kind of. The highly coveted letter from the Ironman Triathlon World Championships in Hawaii arrived, announcing they had picked my name to compete in the 1999 event in Kailua-Kona, Hawaii.

Holy cow! I couldn't believe my eyes when I read it.

It was a fairy tale come true for me. Dad had moved from Newport Beach to Kailuua-Kona right on the Ironman course, and we had watched the race with him several times on our many visits to see him. It is a spectacular event to watch. For years, I had dreamed about going by his place while competing in the race. Since Ironman Hawaii was the official World Championships, qualifying in a prior Ironman race was the only way to get in. Those slots required a level of commitment in training I could not even imagine. However, a lottery was held each year to allow 100 "average Joe" entries into the race. The odds were extremely low (~3 percent), but I kept my dream alive by entering that lottery every year.

My first thought upon seeing the letter was to question how I could possibly find time to do all the necessary training without losing my job, family, or both. A 2.4-mile swim, 112-mile bike ride, and 26.2-mile marathon in the Kona heat would not happen purely by desire. Pulling this off would require a PhD in balance and a *lot* of prayers.

Fast-forward four months later, and things seemed to be falling into place. Despite my global travel schedule, I had read several books, put together a training plan, and executed it with precision. The key was learning how to sneak in my runs and rides (stationary bike) on business trips while making up the swim workouts in my time back home. It did wonders for the jet lag and helped me sleep when my internal clock was off in another time zone. I was starting to feel as if I could do this.

Then Marla said something that changed my paradigm 100 percent. We were discussing making family time a priority on weekends when she blurted:

"If you put as much time into your family as you do into training for this triathlon, we would have no issues."

Gulp.

It stuck, as I knew it was true. I was speechless. And guilty.

Circle of Life

My life had been all about me. Ironman tends to do that to you. Everything I did revolved around my job and triathlon training. There was no time for much else besides the critical sleeping and eating to keep it all going. The family had taken a back seat. I immediately rummaged through my Golden Gate University telecommunications binder and pulled out the Circle of Life.

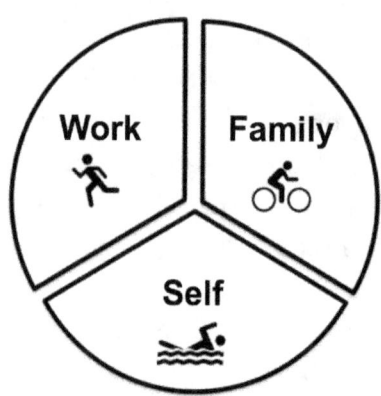

As I mapped it out, it was clear as the light of day. I had been in a cloud of denial and lost perspective in all I had accomplished. Balance had gone out the window the day the congratulatory letter arrived.

Thank God Marla brought me to my senses. A few questions in the Circle of Life quiz convicted me:

- Do you spend "quality" time with your family and children each week?
- Do you make time for regular "date nights" to have quality time with your spouse/partner/children?
- Do you eat dinner as a family at the dinner table three times a week?
- How often do you check email after hours and on weekends without taking the corresponding time off work?

This discussion was much larger than a triathlon, but it helped make the point. Like the three events in a triathlon (swim, bike, run), I needed to find equilibrium in my time and energy for each area of my life (work, family, self). It was as if I was planning to have a stellar swim and bike time while ignoring preparation for the run. My overall performance (a.k.a. my life) would suffer as a result. Or worse, I might not finish the race. I have seen that happen more than once in the triathlon circles, especially in the Ironman distance race. Just like a job, the training can be all-consuming, discarding family members along the way.

Keeping my family a priority would be vital for the rest of my life and something I would model for my children going forward. I had to (and *did*) make changes.

If things go well with the family, life is worth living; when the family falters, life falls apart. This is truer today than ever, underscoring the importance of maintaining balance.

The original Circle of Life quiz made such a profound impact in my life, I revised and personalized it so many times, I have my own version. Here is the Circle of Life quiz (see Appendix III):

www.SurfingForBalance.com/resources

Give it a try.

A balanced life not only feels good, but my experience is it helps those around you too. As the instructor reminded us on the opening day of class:

"If you can keep your life in balance, you will inevitably be a much happier and healthier person."

Mission accomplished.
(L to R, Top to Bottom: Marla, Mike, Grandpa Jack, Matthew,
Marisa)

Race Report

I could write a book about my Ironman experience – it was a dream come true in every way. In 1999, Ironman Hawaii was the official World Championship for professional triathletes. Part of the excitement was starting the race alongside the pros; we all began together with the ceremonial cannon blast in Kailua-Kona harbor. I'll never forget looking Luc Van Lierde, the eventual men's winner that year, in the eye and saying, "Great job" as he passed me on the bike (going in the opposite direction, of course). The biggest thrill, however, was seeing my family on the course as I competed. Both the bike and run courses went right by Dad's place on Alii Drive. I could tell he was choked up as he cheered me on. My entire family, including my father-in-law John D'Zurko, was there to support me. Marisa, our five-year-old daughter, ran the last hundred yards with me, and we crossed the finish line hand-in-hand. It was a thrill of a lifetime for both of us.

Here are three important lessons I learned from Ironman:

1. Over the next 20 years, I completed five Ironman triathlons, spacing them out every couple of years to ensure training

didn't consume my life. Each race required a commitment of eight to 13 hours of training per week for at least 17 weeks – essentially, dedicating an entire summer to the race. The Circle of Life quiz was crucial in maintaining balance between my family commitments and work responsibilities. It kept me on track, enabling me to successfully complete those five races while honoring my obligations.

2. One crucial lesson from those five races was the importance of the bike segment. Both in training and on race day, the bike portion consumed the most time – about 50 percent. Training rides could easily take up an entire day or weekend. To optimize my training, I focused on minimizing time on the bike while maximizing safety amidst distracted drivers. Renting high-quality time-trial bicycles for each race was advantageous, improving my race times and avoiding the costs and logistics of owning and transporting a triathlon bike. This approach also eliminated the need for extensive tools and maintenance.

3. The prayers I recited before, during, and after each Ironman race carried me through to the finish line. I had a ritual of carrying a metal cross with me to keep my focus on Jesus throughout the long day. On the bike, I taped that cross to the end of my tri-bars, which I could see and touch when I was struggling, which was often toward the end of the 112 mile segment. Additionally, I memorized several Bible verses, reciting them as reminders of my trust in God. Here are just a few of those:

"Everything is possible with God" Mark 10:27 (NIV).

"Be still and know that I am God" Psalm 46:10 (NIV).

"Blessed are the poor in spirit, for theirs is the kingdom of heaven" Matthew 5:3 (NIV).

"Ask and it will be given to you" Matthew 7:7 (NIV).

"Nothing at all can ever separate us from God's love"
Romans 8:39 (NIRV).

"I can do all things through Christ who strengthens me"
Philippians 4:13 (NKJ).

Competing at the Ironman level is a great honor and privilege. While you pour your heart and soul (and money) into getting ready for race day, the inherent pride of the Ironman experience is inevitable when one invests so profoundly in physical training. I had an encounter before my inaugural Ironman in Hawaii that truly puts all these aspects into the proper perspective.

Two days before the race, our family was relaxing poolside at Dad's place as our two kids were playing in the water. I watched my son Matthew playing with another boy as I noticed the other boy's father lounging nearby, clearly in shape for the race, with a muscular upper body and dark-tanned skin. With nothing to lose, I began peppering him with questions about the race:

"Are you doing the Ironman?"

"Is this your first?"

"What should I expect for the day?"

The pre-race taper had me feeling pretty secure as this generous man took great care in thoroughly answering all of my questions. I started to feel more confident about the race (my first Ironman) as he made it seem like he hadn't trained any harder than I did. Ha.

As we finished, his wife came over to announce it was time to leave. As our boys said goodbye, he wished me good luck and reminded me of a couple of tips on the swim. I watched his wife walk up behind him with a wheelchair. It had not occurred to me he never moved the lower half of his body during our conversation. As she helped him move from the lounge chair to the wheelchair, I stood there in stunned silence with my mouth surely gaping open, trying to figure out how he was possibly going to do this race without the use of his legs.

That night, I looked up his name and realized I had been talking to a world champion Ironman, Carlos Moleda. Carlos was a former US Navy Seal who had been paralyzed from the waist down in an intense firefight while part of a Navy Seal operation to secure Panama President

General Manuel Noriega in 1989. Nine of the ten men in his unit were wounded, four fatally. Carlos took a bullet in the base of his spine, which paralyzed him for life.

Since then, Carlos has climbed Mount Kilimanjaro, completed the Race Across America (RAAM), and won the Hawaii IRONMAN World Championship *five times*. I will admit to being ahead of him through the bicycle portion of the race, but I will never forget when he passed me early in the marathon. Carlos flew by me before I could even call out his name, ultimately finishing the race nearly an hour ahead of me. Those same two arms that had propelled him in the 2.4-mile swim and 112-mile bike course (with a handcycle) powered him by me in a wheelchair. That experience truly encapsulated what the race is about – it humbled me profoundly.

Physical training is good, but training for godliness is much better, promising benefits in this life and in the life to come.
— 1 Timothy 4:8 (NLT)

11. Peace of Mind

Success is peace of mind which is a direct result of self-satisfaction in knowing you made the effort to become the best of which you are capable.
— John Wooden (UCLA basketball coach)

I love basketball. As a kid, one of the best gifts I ever received was a basketball hoop built in our back alley by our next-door neighbor in CdM. This guy was a carpenter who knew exactly how to construct the perfect backboard and rim onto our garage. For me, shooting hoops became second only to surfing the perfect wave. If I wasn't at the beach, most likely, I was out back perfecting my twenty-foot jump shot. I often dreamed I was Lynn Shackelford of the UCLA Bruins swishing a high-arcing shot from the corner over the power lines in the alley to win the game for UCLA.

One of the more traumatic memories of my childhood could be blamed on my love of basketball. Around age nine or ten, I was shooting away in the midst of a make-believe game when Mom told me to come in because she and Dad were going to the grocery store. I guess I got carried away because when I finally did enter the house from the back door, they were gone. Dad did not like to have to tell us something twice. I cried and cried, not knowing what to do or when they would return. Somehow, I never thought Dad was trying to teach me a lesson. I feared they had left me. When they finally returned, I saw them coming in and immediately ran to the bathroom to wash my face and hide all the tears. Mom knew immediately, and I know she felt horrible for me. I never took any extra shots after that.

I don't have many regrets in life, but quitting the Corona del Mar High School basketball team during my junior year has lingered. I showed up late for a Saturday practice (the surf had been good), and coach Tandy Gillis made sure I would not want to do that again. And I didn't. At the end of practice, I sheepishly told him I was quitting. Enough already. I was 17 years old and didn't need a basketball coach dictating my life.

Or so I thought.

Coach Gillis was a bit of an icon in the basketball world. I appreciate that much more now than I did then. He was an All-American at The University of California at Berkeley (Cal), where he had played under coach Pete Newell, who coached Cal to the 1959 NCAA championship. Rumor had it that Tandy held Jerry West to his lowest offensive point total in his college basketball career at West Virginia University. And if you don't know Jerry West, he was good enough to have the logo of the NBA modeled after him. That year, Tandy's Cal Bears beat Jerry's West Virginia team in the NCAA finals 71-70.

Coach John Wooden

Growing up as a basketball fan in southern California in the 1960s meant you had to be aware of what the Wizard of Westwood (as Coach John Wooden was known) was doing on the basketball court at UCLA. [1] It all started for me when I stayed up late with Dad to watch the KTLA Channel 5 replays of those UCLA games. I could not wait to hear the "Oh MYs" from announcer Dick Enberg as UCLA ran endlessly up and down the court, scoring at will, almost always ending up on the winning side. Dad would surely add that I usually fell asleep by halftime, as the replays started at 11:00 p.m.

The Wooden-coached UCLA Bruins won ten NCAA Men's Basketball Championships over 12 years (1964-1975), including seven in a row (1967-1973), and had four seasons where they went undefeated (1964, 1967,1972, 1973). His UCLA teams suffered only three defeats on their home court at Pauley Pavilion over ten years, amassing a staggering record of 150 wins to just three losses. The consistency of those teams for winning basketball games was epic.

What Coach Wooden was doing was unprecedented in the sports world, and I could not help but get caught up trying to understand it. Something was quite different about how this man approached the game. Amidst the myriad of UCLA victories, he inspired his players to find their very best within themselves while being as cool as a cucumber watching them do it from the sidelines.

Even during the tensest moments of a game, when his team would appear rattled, he would let them play on without calling a timeout. He wanted to let them figure it out. After the game, he was always very humble, giving credit to those around him before allowing the spotlight to shine on him. Most unique of all, Coach Wooden never spoke about "winning" to his players. He focused on helping each player become the best they could be on the court, as well as off. He emphasized the importance of practice, telling his players that the games would go well if they practiced well. "Failing to prepare is preparing to fail."

Fast forward 20 years from those days to Silicon Valley in 1992, and Coach Wooden's model for success came back to the forefront of my life. After Siemens purchased ROLM, I stayed with Siemens and soon found myself in the most challenging job I have ever had in my career. Like my time at Covina Hills Racquet Club, the "circle of life" balance went right out the window as I struggled to maintain pace with the Silicon Valley Express I was riding. I was a field sales manager carrying a $6 million annual sales quota for telecommunications systems to the top technology companies in Silicon Valley. Our customer list read like a who's who of Silicon Valley: IBM, Cisco, Netscape, Adobe, H.P., Intel, Microsoft, Lucent, Applied Materials, 3Com, and many more.

I had ten sales representatives reporting to me who fought daily battles for sales territories, new accounts, quota alignment, customer satisfaction, and that elusive purchase order to bring home the deal against our competition. It was an all-out dogfight every day. I began to feel as if I was in over my head. Each day, I went home to my family feeling bloodied and battle-weary. I was struggling to find *any* satisfaction in the midst of it all.

In a panic to find help, I sat down and typed out a letter to Coach Wooden. I knew it was a long shot, yet I was hoping someone might see it and take the time to respond. Wooden had been able to maintain a sense of peace and composure among his team without putting any emphasis on the win. I wanted to know how he did that.

Within one week, I had a *handwritten* letter in a *handwritten* envelope addressed to me from Coach Wooden himself. He didn't even use the self-addressed, stamped envelope I had included.

Huh?

He opened by thanking *me* for taking the time to write:

"Your words of commendation were very kind and deeply appreciated. Many thanks for taking the time to express yourself."

I was aghast. Coach Wooden was demonstrating the principles he taught. He gave me all the resources I needed and more, even including a page of resources with corresponding ISBN numbers (handwritten by him). I soon created a leadership model for my sales team around his "pyramid of success" that drove our team to exceed the sales quota two years in a row while significantly improving customer satisfaction ratings. The model made sense.

"Talent is God-given. Be humble. Fame is man-given. Be grateful. Conceit is self-given. Be careful."

— Coach Wooden

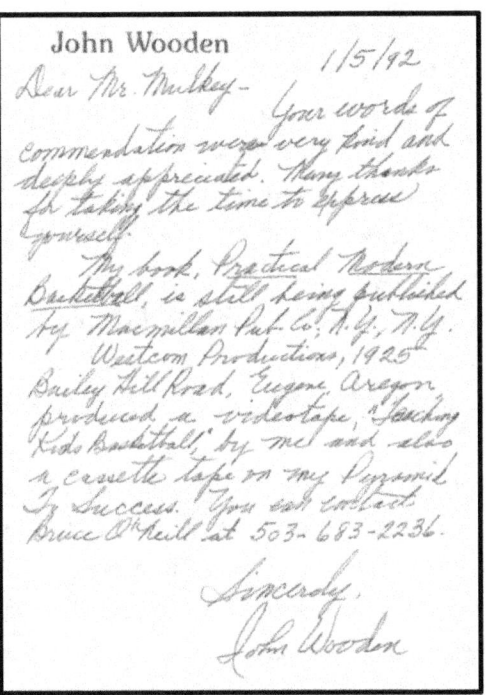

When our two children, Marisa and Matthew, were old enough to play organized basketball, I entered the coaching ranks, determined to make amends for quitting Coach Gillis' team in high school. I modeled my coaching around Coach Wooden's now-famous "pyramid of success," [2] which summarized the building blocks required for success.

I coached youth basketball for 15 years, following our kids up to high school. Integrating Wooden's pyramid into my team brought huge rewards to me, the players, and the parents of the kids I was coaching. Each player was required to learn the pyramid and provide examples of how each block could help us during our games. We even used the appropriate blocks as our team cheer ("1-2-3 CONFIDENCE!!") after a timeout or before a game. I let them tell *me* which block we needed to call out, and they always had suggestions.

When I read Coach Wooden's first book, *They Call Me Coach*, I discovered a crown jewel smack in the middle that had been missing in my analysis of his model for success. Although he seemed to embody Christianity in who he was and how he went about his business, I had never seen him mention his beliefs. Then, in chapter 13, discussing his thoughts on success, Coach Wooden quoted straight from the Bible:

"But seek ye first the kingdom of God, and his righteousness, and all these things shall be added unto you" (Matthew 6:33, NIV).

Right there, Wooden shared the story of his Christian faith and how basketball was of minor importance compared to his faith in our Lord Jesus Christ. He described carrying a metal cross of Jesus in his pocket through all those many games at UCLA so he could hold on to it and be comforted by his Savior when things got difficult during the game. He had rubbed the cross for comfort to the point that it had been worn down on the corners over the years.

Oh MY.

It was so simple, yet so very true. The mere idea of attaining peace of mind through faith in the cross in pursuit of success would be a theme of my career for the next two decades in Silicon Valley. Success is in God's eyes, not the world's. I bought several metal crosses as reminders. Most remarkable of all was that Coach Wooden practiced what he preached. His players all admired him for his principles and commitment to his faith. He really lived it. That set John Wooden apart and helped put into proper perspective the level of success he achieved at UCLA.

As a coach, father, and follower of Jesus Christ as my Lord and Savior, I found Coach Wooden to be an excellent model of the values our holy Bible teaches to children on the basketball court and adults in the business world. It enabled me to go home at the end of the day content that, regardless of how the day had gone, I gave it my best and it now rested in God's hands. The Bible teaches, "The joy of the Lord is your strength" (Nehemiah 8:10). This joy is a quiet confidence, a state of inner peace that can only come from God. Thank you, Mr. Wooden.

The Lord is my strength and my defense; he has become my salvation.
— Exodus 15:2 (NIV)

Notes

1. Wooden authored and co-authored 17 books before he died in 2010 at the age of 99. I have listed a couple of my favorites below. A Google search on "John Wooden" will bring up many more. They all model the values and beliefs of this remarkable man.

   a. *Wooden on Leadership: How to Create a Winning Organization (2005)* by John Wooden and Steve Jamison. Wooden's strategies for competitive greatness translated into a leadership principles book for business or sports, a Wall Street Journal and LA Times bestseller.

   b. *Coach Wooden's Pyramid of Success: Building Blocks for a Better Life (2005)* by John Wooden and Jay Carty. A translation of Wooden's philosophy into a self-help handbook based upon the Pyramid of Success blocks.

   c. *They Call Me Coach (1988)* by John Wooden. This was Wooden's first book and a personal favorite of mine. It describes his humble upbringing on a small farm in Indiana and how his relationship with his father impacted him. It also is the only one of his books that covers the UCLA basketball teams in quite a bit of detail, which I appreciated, having watched so many of those games.

2. Coach John Wooden's "Pyramid of Success" can be found at: https://www.thewoodeneffect.com/pyramid-of-success/

12. HODADS

Don't give up on your dreams, or your dreams will give up on you.
— Coach John Wooden

Life on the Silicon Valley Express seemed to be running smoothly, at least from my perspective. I had mastered the art of striking a sensible equilibrium between the demands of work, personal life, and self-care as I managed software partners for Oracle's hardware systems division in Santa Clara. Guided by the principle of balance, it had become evident that promotions within Oracle were unlikely, a reality I had come to terms with. My primary concern was doing my job well enough to avoid losing it. Rather than dedicating extra hours to climbing the corporate ladder, I found greater value in investing that time at home with my family, contributing to the foundation of a robust future.

When the pace did get too hectic for me, I counted on a trip over the hill to Steamer Lane as my escape route. Doug Haut, the consummate craftsman behind Haut Surfboards in Santa Cruz, tailored a personalized 8'3" tri-fin surfboard explicitly designed for the formidable winter swells at Steamer Lane. Of course, it was a bright fire engine red in the spirit of the red surfboard Eric Hops rode at San Onofre in my youth. Mom also loved the color red. That board carved up those waves like a newly sharpened steak knife. I was in Heaven on it every time I paddled out at Steamers. We aptly named it "Big Red."

When Marla asked me what I wanted for my 50th birthday (many moons ago), my immediate thought was not to give up on my lifelong dream of filming a surfing movie. Ever since the evaporation of our "Mexican Miracle" surf video in Mazatlán (in 1972), the vision of starring alongside my closest surfing bros in a surfing film had persisted. It was a wish I thought could only come true in Heaven.

Yet, the moment Marla granted her approval to film a surf movie, I sprang into action like a kid who had been given the keys to the candy store. You could see it in my eyes; it was finally coming to fruition. I was stoked!

Since my birthday is in January, selecting Steamer Lane as the filming location made perfect sense. Steamer Lane is *the* go-to spot when the rain-soaked Pacific storms bring powerfully consistent surf into Monterey Bay that time of year. Moreover, the location offers an ideal setting for filming from the elevated cliffs, where you can easily perch and capture surfers navigating the waves below. During the last three years in January, I had surfed amazingly consistent 8-foot waves that never seemed to end. I could hardly contain myself; I was giddy with anticipation of what was to come.

The call went out to a few close surfing friends whom I knew would be pumped to join. We booked a cottage at Seascape Resort in Aptos (jacuzzi required) for the birthday weekend and began searching for a cinematographer to film us. I asked each megastar surfer to bring their big wave quiver, a CD of their favorite surf tunes, and photographs to document their history with surfing. I took the project a bit more seriously, anthologizing a 25-page term paper complete with abundant photos and footnotes galore. God lit a fire in me with this project. That term paper turned out to be the genesis of a blog I started in 2014 (surfingforbalance.com). And that blog led to the publishing of this book. Thank you, God.

HODADS (L to R): Jack Schott, John Park, John Davis, Mike Mulkey

The Surfing Celebrities

- Jack Schott – Jack was a former roommate who shared many epic days surfing with me over the years and was my loyal *singles* tennis partner at the John Wayne Tennis Club in Newport Beach. Jack was the best surfer I knew and always seemed to stay out longer and catch more waves than I did, despite having ten years on me. He came down with a horrible cold on our *HODADS* weekend, sitting out the first day, and then borrowing a "deep-dive" wetsuit to get in for some action the second day. He still out-surfed us all. Jack defies all odds by continuing to surf today into his eighties (on a short board).

- John Park – As the founder of Clear Spirit Surfboards, John was part of our CdM community who frequented San Onofre with my dad and me back in the late 1960s when surfing was all we thought about (well, almost). Johnny led me on surfing adventures in Baja back in the seventies and eighties and was a member of the infamous "Mexican Miracle" trip to Mazatlán in 1972, where we inadvertently exposed all of our video films. Johnny is the one Christian I knew who ushered me to church on the first day in Newport Beach when I arrived in a suit and tie.

- John Davis – John was my only surfing bro from Silicon Valley (Sun Microsystems). Ten years my senior, John and his wife Deb built their dream surf chalet on 38th Street in Santa Cruz, including a quiver room for surfboards and a hot outdoor shower with a bench seat to help extract the wetsuit. I am eternally indebted to them for that shower; it is the only way I can get out of my wetsuit on a cold winter day at Pleasure Point. John became the highlight of the hotel room filming of Hodads surf stories with his quick wit and humor. My favorite line at the end of his talk: "Thank you very much. I'm here all week. Try the buffet."

- Gary Irving – Gary was a rare find as a local Santa Cruz artist/photographer who joined us as our *HODADS* cinematographer and producer. He was an answer to my prayers. Gary immediately understood what we were trying to accomplish with the movie. Considering the incredibly flat surf that weekend, he invested untold hours into the final production, giving it the vital spark it needed. Gary did a spectacular job producing what will be remembered as the surf movie to end all surf movies. I lost touch with him shortly after our film was produced. Unbeknownst to us, later that year, in 2005, Gary married actor Paul Newman's daughter, Nell Newman. He never mentioned that one.

HODADS was filmed on the weekend of January 14, 2005. [1] Despite some serious objections from the surfing celebrities, I held firm on naming it HODADS, a surfing term that describes a surfer without much skill. When you bring together five surfers whose combined ages cover more than 270 years, it would be serious HODAD surfing, whether we wanted to admit it or not. The title stuck.

As luck would have it, we had a freak lull in the surf in Santa Cruz for the entire weekend. Steamer Lane was so flat not a single surfer was in the water on Saturday, which is unheard of during January. I could not believe our luck. We decided to invite Gary and his camera into our Seascape cottage with unlimited pizza and beer to spend Saturday recording each of us recalling our glory days of growing up with surfing. We had many laughs jabbing at each other as we took our turn on camera. On Sunday, Gary let us in on a secret spot in Monterey Bay that "always had surf." He was right. On Sunday, we filmed a few decent surf sessions at that secret spot, which Gary masterfully turned into a surfing movie.

HODADS was a lifelong dream come true for me. It turned out better than I could have wished, largely because of the extra time we had to film each of our personal histories with surfing. God had his hand in that. Those scenes Gary filmed in our hotel room are a treasure for us to pass on to the next generation. The whole event was about being stoked with good friends, sharing precious memories, and enjoying God's magnificent creation in the process.

In 2015, we held an informal 10-year reunion of *HODADS* to rekindle some of that good karma and watch a rerun of the movie. We all agreed that we looked *a lot* younger on film ten years ago. Lol. We ended up having an expensive hamburger at the Spanish Bay Inn at Pebble Beach while our boards were neatly strapped on the roof of our van, poised for action. The two 70-year-olds in the group assured me that not surfing that day had nothing to do with our age.

Right.

In the end, I can now rest peacefully on Earth, knowing I finally got my lifelong dream of a surf movie. God is good.

Then, like a lightning strike, at the age of 62, my world turned upside down.

———————————————

Come to me, all you who are weary and burdened, and I will give you rest.
— Matthew 11:28 (NIV)

Note

1. The full-length DVD Gary Irving produced is available for special order through "surfingforbalance.com" (click "Contact Mike"). An abbreviated version of the full-length DVD is available for viewing online at:

   https://surfingforbalance.com/2018/07/18/hodads-the-movie/

   Part I - HODADS (the "surfing"): 10:40

   Part II - HODADS (the "surf stories"): 12:50

4th Wave – Stoked!

- Excited about my future as I paddle into new territory.

13. New Beginnings

God doesn't ask us to be successful, only faithful.
— Amish Proverb

As much as I had been anticipating it, I was seriously wounded when the words finally came. After 25 years of continuous employment in Silicon Valley, the layoff bullet I had been dodging for so many years finally caught me in January of 2017. The official explanation was "corporate downsizing." The farewell email below went out that afternoon, nine minutes before I officially ended my career at Oracle:

> January 19, 2017 (3:51 pm):
>
> Subject: New Beginnings
>
> I will be leaving Sun/Oracle effective today – time for new beginnings!
>
> It has been my very great pleasure to work with you all.
>
> THANK YOU – especially to Vijay Tatkar, who has been my inspirational & loyal leader these past few years.
>
> Going forward, I look forward to staying in touch with you.
>
> Mike Mulkey

New beginnings, for sure.

I had been through the corporate downsizing exercise more times than I wanted to count. Once the dot-com bubble burst in 2000, layoffs at Sun Microsystems became a drumbeat that never seemed to end. When Oracle Corporation purchased Sun in 2009 for $7.4 billion, everyone was scrambling to justify their existence to our new CEO, Larry Ellison. We were *all* on the chopping block.

It reminded me of a Gary Larson *The Far Side* comic, where one deer says to the other deer (who has a bullseye on his chest):

"Bummer of a birthmark, Hal!"

I grew accustomed to being summoned with my peers before management for the dreaded closed-door session, where one of us would receive the official "adios amigo" speech. Each meeting was preceded by a short-notice email with your appointed time (15 minutes each). We would gather at the coffee station to compare notes on our times. The afternoon was rough as you watched your comrades pack up their belongings and head to the parking lot. It was as if we were being lined up for a firing squad and didn't know who was going to get the bullet in the head.

The layoff meetings had become so commonplace one of my managers actually read me the official "You're fired" script in a closed-door session, only to pause, and then tell me he was kidding. He laughed, but I didn't.

What?

At least I knew how it was going to feel when I finally *did* hear the official script. Thinking it over afterward, I was sorry I hadn't fallen to the floor and faked a heart attack.

All hoodwinking aside, *my* turn came to hear the official news from my boss. I could not help but pause for the joke, but he was *not* kidding. I walked out of his office feeling as if I had a bold "**L**" tattooed across my forehead ("Loser" or "Laid-off," take your pick). As the official script stated, it had nothing to do with my performance, age, or even my daily use of the corporate gym. I had awakened in the wrong job with the wrong product at the wrong time. I shuddered at the thought of not having anywhere to go the following day. The world stopped turning as I walked back to my office down the hall.

The goodbyes on that final day were memorable and many. I usually started my day in the cafeteria, where Mary, Julia, and several other faithful servers had become an important part of my work routine. I would miss those folks.

I then dropped in on the few members of my team who were left to defend the fort. There were lots of hugs and a few tears. Ricarda stopped by my office as I was packing my final box with her cheery "Buenos Dias" to empty my trash. Knowing my limited Spanish, she understood immediately when I motioned the cutthroat sign to her. I handed her one of my plants, and she showed great compassion.

Then, my good friend Steve Sarvate and I sneaked out to our secret private tennis court for a final rally on the Oracle clock. He lost his entire team in the layoff (including his manager) but somehow survived. Steve lasted another two years at Oracle before getting laid off. He then sold his home in Sunnyvale and moved to an apartment in San Francisco. Once the pandemic hit, we had a couple of Zoom calls to check in on each other. We both missed our regular tennis game. He passed away suddenly from a heart attack in 2021 on a tennis court in the city while waiting for a match. Steve read all of my blogs on surfingforbalance.com, and I rest in the comfort that he knew (and often debated with me) the truth of Jesus Christ. God bless him.

As I bid farewell to the Club Oracle recreation center staff after my shower, I was reminded how my officemates could not understand how I found time to go to the gym each day. I would reply I could not understand how they could not. It made an incredible difference in my productivity and attitude at work. But I will admit to knowing the entire recreation staff almost better than I knew my own team.

As I walked out to the parking lot with my boxes, the looks I got from those left behind brought back fresh memories of the times I had been in *their* shoes. The sense of guilt was disconcerting. They would soon bear the burden of picking up the pieces since my work did not disappear.

The day was emotionally draining. Despite trying to be present amid the farewells, I could not help but wonder about my future. A Silicon Valley marketing job would not be easy to land if you were unemployed at my age, no matter how good you were. I'd been told I should try a little Grecian Formula on my hair and maybe a pair of cool-looking eyeglasses.

Okay.

The drive home was a bit more upbeat. Windows rolled down with the sunroof open, there was a feeling of release creeping in on me. I would not lose sleep over the breakup with Oracle CEO Larry Ellison. I sensed this could be good. Maybe even great!

The family and I decided to head straight to the theater for an early showing of the Disney movie *Moana*, which turned out to be the perfect anecdote to the day. It opened with a short film called *Inner Workings*, which immediately spoke to me. *Inner Workings* was a short story about a California technology worker bee named Paul. The movie tracked his internal organs (brain, heart, lungs, stomach, etc.) through a typical day as his co-workers sat at their desks, entering data into their computers.

The employees were moving in monotonous unison while Paul's brain took notice of the dreary routine of his life. He could see this cycle would eventually lead to his death as a sad, miserable, lonely man. Not surprisingly, Paul looked to be my age. Ha. I felt God was suddenly waking *my* internal organs into a new life. I was stepping off the Silicon Valley Express for the first time in years. This refreshing change meant I could now paddle out at Steamer Lane midday during the week. Life didn't get much better than that.

Yeehaw! I was stoked.

At 62 years of age, it was time to go job hunting. I decided to write about it as a means of coping with the ordeal. According to the outplacement firm Oracle Corporation provided to ease my transition, this was good therapy.

Life carried on, even though my job had stopped. In many ways, nothing changed, including the bills. The severance check was nice and looked good on paper. But once I realized it was a lump sum (versus a biweekly deposit), less the taxes and costs for COBRA insurance, I got concerned. For good reason.

For 25 years, I had gone to work to provide all my family needed. I was lost with nowhere to go and no guarantee I could continue as the breadwinner. I needed a plan. Having my calendar open was not the good thing it used to be. I quickly realized the importance of keeping myself busy to stay in a healthy state of mind. Surely, I could land on my feet. All those years of fighting the good battle in the valley of infinite silicon did teach me a thing or two. Work/life balance had been my creed, but I also knew how to handle combat. I was not afraid of digging into a foxhole for a frontline fight to find work.

I experienced days of melancholy when I lacked purpose and realized my job had been how I measured my value. This realization was humbling. I wanted to make some changes. Like Paul in the movie *Inner Workings*, my perspective had changed, and I feared what might lie ahead.

I had been on the express train for 25 years, blowing by all the stops with a total focus on the destination *only*. Suddenly, the train had stopped, and I got off. This unfamiliar territory meant I didn't know my way around town. The Oracle cafeteria and rec center were nowhere in sight. I met new people in the library and the park while eating my homemade sandwiches. I frequented Philz Coffee in Sunnyvale so often I was on a first-name basis with the manager, Travis. He even gave me a free mug one day, which warmed my heart.

The good news was I had sufficient margin in my day to enjoy a rich time of prayer and meditation. Every day. I sensed God had plans for my passion around work/life balance; thinking about what might unfold was exciting. I knew this time away from the daily routine of work was a gift, and I wanted to use it wisely. I studied John Wooden's Pyramid of Success for further encouragement. At the very pinnacle were the two words I committed myself to stand by:

- Faith (Through prayer.)
- Patience (Good things take time.)

As I faithfully waited on God, I recited a prayer each morning by Saint Ignatius Loyola. [1] Its simplicity and purpose were just what I needed to start each day:

Lord Jesus Christ.
All that I have and cherish, you have given me.
I surrender it all to be guided by your will.
Your grace and your love are enough for me.
Give me these Lord Jesus, and I ask for nothing more.
Amen.

For I know the plans I have for you, declares the Lord, plans to prosper you and not to harm you, plans to give you hope and a future.
— Jeremiah 29:11 (NIV)

Note

1. Saint Ignatius Loyola was a sixteenth-century Spanish Catholic priest who founded the religious order of *The Society of Jesus* (*The Jesuits*). He was one of the most influential Roman Catholic figures of his era.

14. The 2X4

No time is lost waiting on God.
— Amish Proverb

My faith and patience were acutely tested following my layoff from Oracle. I put in more hours in the job *search* than I had for my job, only to be told each time I did not make the final cut for landing the job. With each rejection, doubt loomed over me like an ill-fitting garment. Of course, my *age* was at the top of the list. It was hard to hide that. Despite knowing I exceeded the job requirements, my extensive experience seemed to count against me. So, I tried the hair coloring thing and immediately realized I was a fish out of water. I could barely speak without thinking about it self-consciously. And forget the fake glasses. Putting them on made me feel like a con man selling snake oil. In a way, maybe I was.

Regardless, a harsh cloud of doubt set in and followed me around. Living this way was like a long lull of waves in the water as the sun dipped into the horizon. I was getting cold, and yet, I refused to paddle in. Surely, one last set was coming. So, I kept at it, praying hard God had one last big wave coming in for me. I needed a little more patience. Good things take time.

Then, I thought God's providence was delivering my dream job at a data storage company in downtown Mountain View called PureStorage. Not only was the commute a mere stroll from home, but the role perfectly aligned with my expertise in partner marketing. The job listing explicitly favored candidates with Oracle software knowledge – a qualification I possessed in abundance. Moreover, my prior engagement with PureStorage as part of my responsibilities at Oracle provided invaluable connections within the company. I knew this was my job to lose, so I set out to do everything possible to ensure I got the nod.

Through nearly two months of exhaustive effort, I underwent 12 interviews and delivered two formal presentations to senior executives. Despite the intensity, every sign pointed to me as their preferred choice. Additionally, a connection through church at the senior executive level offered further support, reinforcing my conviction God was leading me to PureStorage as my next stop on the express train.

In the end, I had to call *them* to find out they hired someone else. That was a Muhammad Ali shot straight to the forehead. I was on my back out cold. And I never saw it coming. The ten count was long gone before I could find my way back onto my feet, and I was still wobbling. Angry questions for God burst out of me. My patience had worn thin, as had the lump sum severance check from Oracle. My indignant state of panic had plenty of rage mixed in.

As I searched deep in my soul for the right answers, I recalled a recent meeting with a close friend, Roger Williams, who was always so positive and confident in how God is at work in our trials.

Was this rejection the 2×4 Roger had been referring to?

Roger served as the President and CEO of the Mount Hermon Christian Conference Center in the Santa Cruz Mountains. He was also in the midst of an arduous struggle with cancer, yet he continued teaching and providing visionary leadership at Mount Hermon despite his failing health.

My purpose in meeting with Roger was to ask him how he had known it was God's calling when he gave up his successful business career to go into full-time ministry. I had been sensing a personal calling from God away from my business career and knew Roger could help guide me. Although his declining health made it challenging for him, we spent two and a half hours together that evening discussing God's calling for a dramatic change in his life. Roger spoke with an intensity and delight I can't quite do justice to with words. I felt God had ordained our meeting.

Roger's response to my question was crystal clear. He explained God had quite simply hit him over the head with a 2×4 when his calling arrived. The 2×4 was unmistakable. "You will know for sure when it happens to you," he told me.

After hearing his story about his calling to serve, I had to agree. A 2×4 *had* hit him. I left the meeting with great relief that it was not yet time for me. As I drove home over the summit on Highway 17, I praised God for such lucid advice from such a dear friend.

My 2X4

Reflecting on Roger's advice, I still felt dazed and discouraged by the PureStorage rejection. I had shifted my focus to startups since I had all the skills needed for a smaller company environment where each person had to wear many hats (sales, marketing, alliances, product management, product marketing, product development, and more). A good friend set me up to meet with a senior executive from a venture capital company on Sand Hill Road who worked with Silicon Valley startups. He surely could set me straight on how to land a marketing job in this valley.

We met outdoors at Philz Coffee in Palo Alto, and I will never forget the first words out of his mouth (beyond the niceties):

"You'll never get hired in this valley."

I gurgled my sip of coffee, almost getting it down the wrong pipe.

"Uhum. Excuse me?"

He had not even looked at the manila folder I handed him with all my good deeds. I was utterly flabbergasted and did not know what to say. My sales pitch was gone before it even started. The wind had left my sails. No waves were coming. The sun had set – time to paddle in.

His following sentence provided clarity, but still hung in the air like the Hindenburg poised to explode into flames:

"The average age of a CEO in this valley is just over 30, and they are not going to hire you."

That was the only time I can remember not finishing my Philz coffee. I had plenty of adrenaline running through my veins already. And the buzz lasted for days.

Suddenly, Roger's wisdom rang out to me; there was no mistaking the 2×4. The cloud of doubt lifted, and my vision became quite clear. I began to see I had been hit multiple times.

My layoff from Oracle clobbered me with the power of a *steel* 2×4. It shook my foundation. While pursuing the job search and taking classes from the outplacement firm, I sensed my heart was not fully in the work I sought, but I kept ignoring those feelings and thoughts. The fear of unemployment was driving me. The bills still came in, and I needed to find a way to turn the bi-weekly auto deposit back on. That was the lifeline for my family.

Then, each job rejection became another 2×4 slamming into my head, ringing my bell with the message God was calling. This final meeting with the VC guy simply painted the finishing coat of resin on. There was no question in my mind God was redirecting me. At 62, I had somehow outgrown my tenure as a Silicon Valley worker bee. The only question was *where* God was pointing me to ...

With a crucial dose of faith the bills would get paid and considerable patience I could wait 12 months to start a new job, I soon was enrolled in a 1-year training program to become a professional life coach (a New Ventures West Integral Coach). This set a path for me to transition my career from high-tech marketing to helping others navigate Silicon Valley's work/life balance challenges. It was a job made in Heaven for me to go on a mission of self-discovery for my future. I was stoked beyond measure.

New Ventures West (NVW) had the most advanced training curriculum available, with a seasoned faculty known for their wisdom and experience in coaching. I needed the best to effectively lead people in a discussion about balancing priorities in Silicon Valley. The training felt right. I was sure God was in it.

That year was a fantastic transformation of my self-identity as I looked deep inside to find my passage forward. I was coached in the class by professional instructors *and* fellow students to help me understand the experience my clients would have as I coached them. Learning to slow down and listen with my heart to understand what was going on deep inside *me* was key. For someone riding the express train in Silicon Valley for 25 years, the learning was unsettling. My world had been all about going *faster*, not slower. I could feel this new train was on the right track even though it took the entire year to adjust. I was finally following my heart. This was life-changing stuff. May all the glory go to God for leading me there. And of course, I'm still learning.

Hearing from Heaven

Roger Williams went to his heavenly home on September 14, 2014, succumbing to cancer he called "his insidious dance partner." His passing came just a few days after his 21st anniversary at Mount Hermon. Praise God for the gift I received to be with Roger and drink from the deep well of wisdom he offered.

Roger walked through life here on Earth with the exhilaration of his salvation as if walking on Heaven's precipice. He truly glowed as a living example of how the Scriptures can guide and transform you. Nothing speaks louder to me than a life like Roger's, transformed by what God offers.

Roger Williams (1947-2014)

While I was very sad to lose Roger as a friend and mentor here on Earth, I feel closer to him than ever and rejoice at the thought of joining him in Heaven. We will have a great deal more time together in eternity than we did here on Earth. I look forward to that.

Roger was one of the first people to get me excited about Heaven. He spoke of it as if he had been there. I can still hear his voice calling out on the shores of Lake Tahoe as the sun was painting its portrait across the deep blue lake and majestic mountains around it:

"Folks, we can count on God's promise that Heaven will far surpass this beauty we see now.

If you think the colors are good now – wait till you see them in Heaven.

If you think the sunsets are good now – wait till you see them in Heaven

If you think this is a beautiful place to live now – wait until you see it REDEEMED in Heaven!"

Roger's family posthumously published a book he had been working on before his passing. The book appeared on our kitchen counter one night when I arrived home late after the family had gone to bed. I had not known about it and was stunned. I could only imagine Roger ensured its delivery to comfort me. Earlier that night, I had been teaching a group of young adults at our church about Heaven. I got goosebumps when I saw the book:

Hearing from Heaven: A Memoir of God at Work at Mount Hermon

by Roger Williams

Many are the plans in a person's heart, but it is the Lord's purpose that prevails.
— Proverbs 19:21 (NIV)

15. Slow Down

For fast-acting relief, try slowing down.
— Lily Tomlin (American actress & comedian)

Slowing down in Baja California with my surfing bros at Punta
Pequeña, circa 1980

When I think of slowing down, I return to the 1980s and our surfing trips to Punta Pequeña in Baja, California, with good friends John Chick, Eddie Means, John Park, and Peter Vanderburg. As my career was ramping up, those trips taught me to take my foot off the gas pedal and listen within. It was all about slowing down.

Punta Pequeña is a dream of a surfing destination – especially if you catch a solid south swell. This is the kind of surfing spot I dream about finding in Heaven, composed of a perfectly sculpted series of right points that corral south swells as good as anywhere on the California coast. The shallow volcanic rock shelf was perfectly designed for surfing, enabling long rides across endless faces with plenty of room for cutbacks. For a regular foot surfer riding a yellow Hanifin Bananafin longboard (that be me), it was Heaven on Earth. I could not wipe the smile off my face the entire time we were there. The quality of the wave and the length of the ride were unequaled in my surfing experience. Rumor had it you can ride over one kilometer on a really big south swell. Best of all, we were removed entirely from the SoCal mainstream surfing scene. Crowds in the water were not something we had to concern ourselves with, mainly due to the difficulty of getting there.

Punta Pequeña in the 80s was a thousand miles from nowhere, in one of the more remote and inaccessible regions of Baja California. The trip began with a two-day adventure on the rugged but paved Baja Mexico Highway 1, which, for safety reasons, we never drove at night. Then the real trip started.

After 900 or so miles of slugging it out on the pothole-ridden asphalt segment, a clandestine Baja-dusty dirt road appeared out of nowhere (with no signs) to lead us onto the final exam for our driving odyssey. Sixty miles of ungraded rocky, dusty, and, at times, washboard dirt and sand led directly west to the sleepy fishing village of San Juanico, nestled into a point of land sticking out into the Pacific Ocean.

Unless you were driving an army tank, making it up this final section of road was never a sure thing, even if you *had* made it before. It was a full-on assault that included rolling all windows up (with no A/C), putting on a mouth guard to protect your teeth, turning the music up to full volume, and plowing forward at 25 miles per hour while praying you don't get a flat tire or have engine trouble. Removing parts of the car along the way was not uncommon.

To this day, I lay claim to one of the greatest driving achievements in Mexican surfing history with my 1983 VW Diesel Rabbit. When we pulled onto the bluff at Punta Pequeña (with a mere 12 inches of ground clearance), the other surfers looked at us as if we had just landed the Eagle Lunar Landing Module. It had been a new car when we left, but it aged 20 years on that trip. Of course, we never confessed we had paid "mucho dinero" to some local ranchers to tow us through a few sand dunes. It was another Mexican Miracle when they showed up in a large truck with a towing rope. My Rabbit was digging into the sand like a sand crab looking for cover.

Eddie and John christening the 60 miles ahead to San Juanico.
("Dónde está la playa?")

Once camp was established, life at Punta Pequeña settled into a singular focus on surfing. Everything we did was in preparation for the next session in the water. If the surf dropped, we had plenty to keep us busy, but hardly ten minutes went by without a glance at the waves to see if conditions were changing for the next surf session.

If you weren't surfing, you sat in a beach chair drinking beer, scientifically analyzing the tide and wind conditions as the sun lazed across the powder-blue Baja sky. The only responsible duty was rotating the 20 cases of beer into the four ice chests to ensure we had cold brew for the entire trip. It was not as easy as it sounds. Extended games of Bocci ball down the vast, endless beach were the usual diversion in the afternoon if the surf had blown out. But we could only wander a mile or so away for fear the beer would run out, and we would suffer dehydration which could impact the next surfing session.

Looking back on those trips today, I realize my ability to slow down was about the absolute freedom I experienced being so wholly removed from civilized interruptions in my life. Zero connections to the outside world meant my mind and body were in a state of total peace. Backpackers can experience a similar peace on extended trips into the wilderness. We were unencumbered and free, which bonded us with our surroundings. The vast nothingness of the environment soothed my soul in a way I can only dream about today. I could sit in my beach chair and gaze down upon the endless spit of land as far as the eye could see. The beauty was beyond words. Those trips fed my soul in ways only God can explain.

I thirst for the same level of contentedness today.

Going Too Fast

Fast forward to Silicon Valley 40 years later: Our world is moving *too fast*. My vision of the "leisure society" was reduced to rubble by the explosive growth of computers. The chasm between our life today and what I experienced at Punta Pequeña in the 80s looks like the Grand Canyon. Our ability to set aside time to be at peace and rest our souls is like a mirage. Busyness has consumed us, and information technology is bombarding us with an incessant need for our electronic devices instead of focusing on the present moment. The speed is too much for our human psyche to make sense of. Yet, faster and faster we go.

There is a dichotomy here. I love doing so much in so little time with today's technology; I'd be lying to tell you otherwise. I have an iPhone and use it constantly to stay in touch. I can check the surf, tide tables, traffic conditions and view a live camera of Steamer Lane, all with a finger tap on my phone *while* shopping from my electronic grocery list at Trader Joe's. I can even communicate with a family member anytime from anywhere.

That's fantastic.

Yet, like groceries, it comes at a cost.

Dr. Richard Swenson, author of the best-selling book *Margin*, puts it this way:

> The world has witnessed almost continuous change, but never before with such levels of speed, suddenness, complexity, intensity, information, communication, media, money, mobility, technology, weaponry, and interconnectedness.

Let's add "stress" to that list.

Unfortunately, our children are the innocent victims of this onslaught. We have all heard the stories because they are happening to *our* kids. Understandably, they have issues coping with the complexity and speed of life. The statistics are staggering. The issues headline the news every day. Stress, anxiety, depression, lack of sleep, ADHD, obesity, learning disabilities, social skills, and even death from suicide have been linked to the technology overload our children face today.

Here's a simple example. Last week, I received an email from a security service I subscribe to called LifeLock. The subject was "Data Breach Notification," urging me to change my passwords as a preventative measure of the breach. Okay. I went into my password manager program (on my iPhone) to discover I had *263 passwords*. That stressed me out (and still does). I don't think we can begin to understand the toll this stress takes.

My parents both smoked cigarettes as they came into adulthood. It was cool to have a cigarette back then, and they had no good reason not to smoke. Then, they got addicted. Nobody had studied the link between smoking tobacco and deaths from things like lung cancer or emphysema. My mom died of emphysema at age 76. Those studies are out now. But for Mom, it was too late.

Forty years later, I am sure similar studies are forthcoming on the deadly effects of the technological overload we are subjected to today. Our brains are not equipped to handle the barrage of information and radio frequency exposure coming at them. It's too much. The negative impact on our health is clear.

This story is just one example from a close friend of mine:

After high school, his son hit a rough patch in life and developed a serious alcohol/drug habit. It was not pretty, but he got into a long-term rehab center and is doing fantastic. He told me a story about a small group discussion with a dozen other young adults in the same situation while he was in the rehab center. The leader asked each group member what they thought had led to their addiction. *Each of them* agreed it was their deep internal need to *slow down*. Life was moving too fast, and they could no longer cope, so they began to take alcohol or drugs to help them deal with it.

If I were to boil down my 12 months of New Ventures West training to the most important thing I learned, it would be the need for us *all* to *slow down*. Slowing down is a mandatory first step if one genuinely wants to discover and pursue who they are.

I had the opportunity to slow down when I was laid off from my job. It was a bit like Punta Pequeña; suddenly, I had time just "to be." That experience led me to step off the Silicon Valley Express to make a significant transition in my career. I began to feel the freedom one experiences when listening to your heart. It was like going surfing without a leash. I felt empowered to experience the freedom of who I was deep inside without being tethered to earthly expectations. Although I was scared I would fall and lose my way, this new awakening brought a sense of joy not felt in years.

As I began to coach clients, I quickly learned getting them to slow down was the key to my success. Coaching a client traveling through life at today's "normal" speed is like trying to diagnose car trouble with no dashboard to display the metrics. You might as well be throwing darts blindfolded – you have no idea what the underlying issues are. The speed and intensity of life today seem to require losing touch with our inner selves. We are too busy to look at our dashboard.

Meditation is an excellent first step for slowing down. It's remarkable what insights our mind, body, and heart can impart when we grant ourselves the gift of stillness. Most of us tend to see the world in a *physical* sense. If I look okay, I must be okay. Coaching helped me realize there is an equally important *spiritual* side to our being. The soul requires as much attention and care as our physical bodies do. In a sense, we care for our soul when we meditate. The Bible echoes this sentiment with over 60 references to meditation. Praying to God can be a part of that. Praying is a two-way conversation. We quiet ourselves to *listen* as much as (or more than) we do by speaking to God about our needs. I have found those times when I can still my soul before God to be the richest conversations of all.

Learning to pay attention to this exact moment you are in now is a valuable tool for dealing with stress. "Being present" is a phrase for nonjudgmentally allowing yourself to experience the here and now. Another common term is mindfulness, which refers to bringing one's attention to experiences occurring in the present moment. Life-altering awareness can emerge from paying attention to the present moment. Even if it starts with just five minutes a day, mindfulness can make a notable difference. There is a wealth of books on this subject. Two of my favorites are mentioned below. [1]

Looking to Heaven

Five-time Grammy award winner Steven Curtis Chapman was on to something when he released the hit song "Next 5 Minutes" in 1999. The song talks about living the next five minutes as if they were your last five minutes, truly living in the moment.

What if the next five minutes *are* all you have?

I did a great deal of contemplation about my life following the layoff from Oracle and the subsequent one-year sabbatical to become a life coach. There was no question about the 2×4 hitting me square on the head; I could feel God at work in my life. Yet, I found my mind often drifting to my mortality. Mom and Dad were now gone, so I was next, right? Avoiding this reality was kind of difficult. The odds were about 100 percent.

On one hand, this awareness fueled my determination to scale what David Brooks refers to as the "second mountain" in his book, *The Second Mountain.* I saw an opportunity to infuse greater purpose into this new chapter of my journey. Transitioning from the tech industry to coaching, I embraced the freedom of aligning with God's plan for my life. This shift brought with it a profound sense of fulfillment, a guiding light amidst the uncertainties of providing for my family. Yet, it was far from a guaranteed success.

An even weightier question loomed beyond that. The reality of my mortality felt uncomfortably close. Surely more than five minutes away, the end of my life here on Earth *was* closer than I wanted to admit. Life went by so very fast. This awareness only fueled my yearning to live authentically, reminiscent of the freedom I experience when I go surfing without a leash.

Be still before the Lord and wait patiently for him;
— Psalm 37:7 (NIV)

Note

1. Two books I recommend on meditation:

    Altered Traits: Science Reveals How Meditation Changes Your Mind, Brain, and Body by Daniel Goleman and Richard Davidson

    More books than I can count extoll the many wonders of meditation. I liked this book because Daniel and Richard sifted through the morass of clinical research to distill the truth about what meditation can do for us and how to get the most out of it. I had the opportunity to meet Daniel Goleman at a promotional event for this book, and I can assure you he is legitimate.

    Care of the Soul by Thomas Moore

    This is a beautifully written account of how to care for our innermost being. Having a firm belief our soul is what we take with us in the life hereafter, I found this to be a refreshing view on making the most of my life here on Earth in preparation for our eternal home in Heaven. I completely agree with Mr. Moore's assertion that "loss of soul" is a significant problem we face today, resulting in many societal ills. The primary takeaway underscored the profound value of quiet time and meditating daily. According to Mr. Moore, when our inner sense of who we are flourishes due to the way we live, we care for the soul.

16. "We Don't Do Email ..."

Man sacrifices his health in order to make money, then sacrifices his money to recuperate his health.
— Dalai Lama

One of my greatest joys in leaving the tech industry was terminating my email account at Oracle. Enough already. That was another leash I did *not* mind removing. As a marketing manager, I performed most of my job through email. I managed independent software vendors (ISVs) who ran their software on Oracle systems. These ISVs were worldwide, so emails flew into my inbox around the clock. Only on Saturdays did I find a brief respite when Asia and Europe reached a temporary standstill. Yet, the deluge resumed on Sunday afternoon, demanding my constant vigilance to avoid any missteps with crucial partners.

I love email and what it enables. But I hate it more than I love it. My brain was not made to operate in this way. Even without my tech job, I can't seem to avoid using email. But I did find a way to keep myself from being enslaved to it. Working at Trader Joe's (TJ's) has been a game-changer. During my interview, I was informed, quite simply, "We don't do email at Trader Joe's."

Are you kidding me? How can a company survive in today's information-driven economy without email? A Freakonomics podcast titled "Should America Be Run By ... Trader Joe's?" [1] hinted that they are doing quite well *without* email and without many other things grocery store chains accept as modus operandi. I believe TJ's is on to something.

Most of us would agree society would be better off slowing down and incorporating more rest. Much of the chaos and many societal ills we see today can be attributed to our overload. Dr. Richard Swenson nailed it in his 2004 best-selling book, *Margin,* [2] referring to the space that once existed between ourselves and our limits. To take away that space is like reading a book without margins. You won't get very far. Today we are exceeding our limits because our lives have no margins.

Email is a classic margin-eater. It devours our free time and creates a continuous 24/7 flow of information spewing data like a fire hose in full force with nobody holding the nozzle. A small amount may hit the target, but most is wasted water, causing grief and exhaustion for all involved. We all have experienced how email has invaded our personal lives and at work. Even a brief vacation can result in an avalanche of emails, enough to make one regret ever leaving. At Oracle, I frequently returned from vacation to a backlog of a thousand or more emails awaiting my attention.

Just under 40 years ago, we were not doing email at work. It had not been invented. Looking back now, it was heavenly. Email first entered my work environment in the mid-1980s as I launched my high technology career at ROLM Corporation. We worked hard at ROLM without email. Yet when I left the office to come home, I was truly done. My work stayed at the office.

When IBM purchased ROLM in 1984, we were introduced to IBM's PROFS (Professional Office System), IBM's first email system. Most of us viewed PROFS as a joke. It simply relayed information from IBM corporate, which had minimal impact on my day-to-day duties. It was like reading Morse code intended for the Navy when you were in the Army. I could go weeks without checking my inbox and often made fun of those (primarily management) who seemed to spend an excessive amount of their day doing it. Little did I anticipate its evolution into the monster it became.

By the time I left Oracle 25 years later, I spent about two-thirds of my day navigating email. The volume was suffocating. Even in meetings, I was only half-listening as I browsed my "urgent" messages. Like the Peanuts character Pig-Pen, who lived with a cloud of dust, email became a haze that followed me home and on my vacations. The next thing I knew, improvements to the cell phone networks were delivering email to my phone. Holy cow, I could send emails while sitting on the KT22 chairlift at Squaw Valley while surveying my next ski run ("Hey Mark, is my tax return ready yet?"). It seemed to be getting out of control.

Trader Joe's

Leaving Oracle and my email inbox behind was an answer to prayer, but Marla and I still needed to pay our bills. As I mentioned, the bi-weekly auto-deposit from Oracle had stopped, but the bills kept coming (and coming …). Insurance was at the top of that list, as COBRA health insurance [3] is expensive. As we explored options, I decided to go to our local Trader Joe's to complete a job application. As far as I could tell, they had a good insurance package that would enable us to drop our COBRA policy. I had no idea what the job entailed other than bagging a few groceries and putting out some produce. And who didn't like Trader Joe's?

After phoning the store for instructions, I was informed no appointment was necessary. They told me to come down in person and fill out the application; they wanted to meet me. The job application was quick – it only asked for my *high school* education. What. I could leave those college degrees behind. This should be fun.

Suddenly, I found myself perched on a milk crate in the back alley of the store as trucks and cars zoomed by. Amelia (the captain of the store) was probably half my age and dressed in a cheerful Hawaiian aloha shirt with a cheerful smile. I immediately took to her. We were having a nice chat when she inquired about my availability for work. Our discussion went something like this:

> Amelia: "I think you're a good fit for Trader Joe's. When would you be available to work?"
>
> Mike: "That is complicated for me. Could I send you an email on the days and times?"
>
> Amelia: "We don't do email at Trader Joe's."
>
> Mike: "Excuse me?"
>
> Amelia: "We don't do email at Trader Joe's."
>
> Mike [extending my hand to shake]: "When can I start?"

Those words were music to my ears. Without hesitation, I decided to give it a try. With over six years under my belt at the store, I can truthfully say I've cherished every single day. When I clock out at the end of my shift, a sense of contentment washes over me, knowing I've poured my heart into my work and can return home with a deep satisfaction (and fatigue) for a job well done. Whatever tasks remain are seamlessly picked up by the next shift. I find myself working harder yet resting more deeply than in years past.

Come payday, a TJ's Mate (manager) personally delivers my paycheck with a sincere *thank you*. It may be missing a digit or two from my tech days, but the culture at TJ's has won me over. As a life coach, I've come to appreciate the profound value of laughter and joy throughout the day. It's a glimpse of what I imagine work in Heaven to be like.

Here are my top ten reasons I like working at TJ's:

1. "We don't do email . . ."

When I enter the store, I turn off my phone. No email. If we need to communicate, we go face-to-face or ring bells. It is refreshing. I have more margin.

2. We're on a ship.

We're all at sea on a ship in the South Pacific at TJ's. Our jobs are crystal clear to keep our boat on course. One captain (button aloha shirt), a couple of mates (different aloha shirts), and the rest of the crew members (crew member T-shirts) communicate by ringing bells that allow us to be "armed to the teeth" to react to our customers' needs on a moment's notice. Our goal is to "wow" our customers. It's that simple.

3. Variety is the spice of life.

Every employee shift is segmented into eight hourly blocks, each assigned to a distinct task within the store. At the stroke of each hour, we all seamlessly transition to a new assignment. Throughout a single eight-hour shift, I undertake many responsibilities to maintain the store's inventory, organization, cleanliness, and profitability. It sounds straightforward (and it is), but it makes my days fly by and has helped me learn the entire store operation. This brilliantly efficient system keeps me engaged the whole day.

4. Huddles.

Meetings (called "huddles") are five-minute stand-up gatherings in the back galley to communicate important news about keeping things "ship shape" in the store. There is no muss, no fuss. Quick and simple instructions, some good food and grog to sample, and then all hands back on deck to help "wow" our customers. The tech world could learn a lot from this one.

5. Fist bumps, handshakes, and hugs.

Each day at TJ's, I'm greeted with fist bumps, handshakes, and hugs from my fellow crew members – gestures that persist as we part ways at the end of a shift. This tradition remained steadfast even during the challenges of COVID-19. It surprised me at first. If I were to exhibit this behavior at Oracle, I might end up at the HR office. During the first couple of shifts I experienced this, I thought these folks giving out hugs and fist bumps were leaving the company. Yet, I've come to realize these gestures work wonders for morale, fostering a sense of unity and support among the team.

6. Happy people.

TJ's strategy for success is clear: Their employees are on top. They call it the inverted pyramid. When the employees are happy, they take care of the customers. That makes the customers happy. I am happy to work there. It's "hunky-dory."

7. Community.

When I started at TJ's, I wondered why they hired me. Then I saw others they hired and wondered why they hired them. It's like American Youth Soccer (AYSO), where everyone plays. It's one big happy community. There is no A-team and B-team. They even employ people with special needs who work alongside the rest of us. It gives those individuals a great sense of pride to be a part of TJ's community, and the benefits to everyone are enormous.

8. Youth is king.

Many of my co-workers are my young adult children's age (or younger). They are fun, energetic, and full of fascinating insights into life. Most of them have other jobs, school, or both. They are all "gung-ho" to make a future for themselves. They talk to me like I am one of them. At TJ's, *I am* one of them. It's a kick.

9. Hard (physical) work.

Trader Joe's business model is about a high volume of transactions to attain *very* low prices. I soon discovered the considerable amount of physical labor involved in accomplishing that day in and day out. Like the pyramids in Egypt, it all happens one block at a time. The physical effort to move all that product in the back door and out the front door is significant. I walk an average of 4 miles and lift an untold amount of weight every day in the store. I have never felt better. I'm getting paid to go to the gym.

10. Just be you.

TJ's tells you they hired you because of who *you* are, not who they want you to be. So, the word on deck is to "be yourself." For those who know me, that is dangerous. I wear shorts and my Hoka running shoes to work daily, and I love dressing up for the holidays.

Do nothing from selfish ambition or conceit, but in humility count others more significant than yourselves.
— Philippians 2:3 (ESV)

Notes

1.   Podcast: "Should America Be Run by . . . Trader Joe's?"

    https://freakonomics.com/podcast/should-america-be-run-by-trader-joes-ep-359-rebroadcast/

2.   Swenson, Richard A., MD. Margin: Restoring Emotional, Physical, Financial, and Time Reserves to Overloaded Lives. Colorado Springs, CO: NavPress, 1992.

3.   "The Federal COBRA Act gives workers and their qualified dependents the right to continue paying for their workplace health insurance if that coverage would end due to a qualifying event."
    https://www.cobrainsurance.com/what-is-cobra-insurance/

17. Surfing Without a Leash

I wish I'd had the courage to live a life true to myself, not the life others expected of me.
— Bronnie Ware (author of The Top Five Regrets of the Dying)

While the world's first microprocessor [1] was catalyzing the personal computer revolution in Silicon Valley in 1971, the sport of surfing was forever changed by the invention of the surf leash. I was a sophomore in high school when I first saw a surf leash in action while surfing at Swami's Beach in Encinitas. I was stupefied. Tying your foot to your surfboard with a rubber cord virtually eliminated all repercussions of wiping out on a wave. It seemed criminal to me. Yet it quickly became a de facto standard for surfers, helping drive a significant transformation of the sport over the next decade. Most in the water today have never surfed *without* a leash.

Before the leash, surfing not only mandated good swimming and paddling skills, but also required a more cautious approach to the wave you were riding. If you fell and lost your board, the backlash could include a long swim (after some cussing), paddling back out against incoming waves, and potentially an afternoon in your garage doing ding repair (if rocks or other surfboards got involved). Growing up surfing in the 1960s included a *lot* of swimming, paddling, and ding repair. I even got pretty good at body surfing to chase after a lost board. That was how we learned.

Pat O'Neill, son of acclaimed wetsuit inventor Jack O'Neill, is generally acknowledged for inventing the modern surf leash in 1971. [2] In those days, a lost board at Steamer Lane in Santa Cruz meant almost certain death on the rocks, so it is easy to understand his motivation. The surf leash is also how Jack O'Neill lost his left eye. The earlier versions were made from a coiled surgical cord that shot the board back like a bullet after a wipeout. *Ouch!* I imagine Jack's injury impacted the development of leash prototypes in a hurry.

The surf leash helped spawn an avant-garde generation of shortboard surfers fashioning a new style of surfing that required minimal foot movement on the board and maximum body language above the waist. Suddenly, the hot surfers were wiggling like a hula-hooper to slash and tear up and down the face of the wave on boards barely any taller than they were. No penalty existed for trying something beyond your ability, as you could immediately try it again. The result was a dramatic shift in what became possible on a wave.

However, the surf leash did have its skeptics. For those who had grown up surfing longboards without a leash in the 1960s, this major innovation to the sport was not all good news. If you liked freely walking up and down the board while riding a wave, strapping on the leash was analogous to attaching a ball and chain to your leg. Mobility on the board was limited, as you tended to tangle or step on the cord with your bare feet if you did move.

The leash also negated the thrill of trying *not* to fall while riding a more challenging section of a wave. There were no severe consequences to falling, so why not try something crazy? Kicking out of a wave was a technically advanced skill before the leash (with longboards). With the leash, a swan dive was now just as effective in exiting a wave. I likened it to the safety net for the flying trapeze artists at the circus. The success of any given move did not look so formidable once you realized they weren't going to die if they fell.

We quickly labeled it the "kook cord" and agreed among our inner circle *not* to use it. Most troublesome was the increased crowd, as nobody had to swim in for their board if they fell. Suddenly, people were surfing waves they had no right to surf. Getting outmatched by a wave and paying the price with a swim to shore and paddle back out was not only good tutoring but also great for those in the lineup waiting for the next set. At a place like San Onofre, it could take 30 minutes for someone who had lost their board to reappear in the lineup.

My daughter Marisa navigating the rock dance with her leash at San Onofre

However, it soon became apparent I would lose quickly in the game of improving my surfing if I went without it. *That* caught my attention. Of course, I wanted to be the best surfer in the water, and there was no denying the leash gave you more time to ride waves. As soon as I noticed someone pass me with a new maneuver, I caved in and sheepishly strapped the shackle onto my ankle. Ugh.

When wave and crowd conditions allow, I sometimes paddle out without a leash. A sense of freedom and excitement immediately washes over me. It's like removing the seat belt and rolling down the windows in my car on a bluebird day. Caution is in the air, but I feel free as a bird. Nostalgia sets in. This is how surfing was meant to be. There is an excitement of risk in trying to "hang five," knowing I could lose contact with my board by falling. I can move up and down the board without fear of getting tangled. My surfboard becomes a part of me I hold onto at all costs. The stoke of a long ride without a leash takes on greater joy, lifting me to kick out with a howl. My soul is awakened in triumph. It takes me back to my roots and reminds me how the ocean has been a part of my growing and learning as a human being. One day, I will look back and realize each wipeout and subsequent swim to shore was a part of God's plan for my life, preparing me for the ultimate ride in Heaven.

Taking off the Leash in Life

After 25 years in several high-tech sales and marketing jobs in Silicon Valley, my life had taken a big turn to become a *New Ventures West Integral Coach*® (a life coach). At our graduation, we each had a moment to express what those 12 months meant. My summation of the year in training was that it taught me how to surf without a leash. Unleashing the security of my high-tech job (and paycheck) gave me the freedom to live a more genuine life than the world expected of me. I had discovered how riding the Silicon Valley Express had me so wound up each day I lost track of who I was. I didn't have time for that.

A big part of learning to be a life coach was being present. For me, that meant slowing down – a *lot*.

Amid my busyness, I saw life passing me by. I was checking off all the boxes to earn a living, support my family, and care for my health. Yet, in the struggle, I lost touch with who I was. The New Ventures West coaching program allowed me to paddle out without my leash. A new awareness began to wash over me. It was refreshing and yet challenging as I entered the unknown.

What I had experienced was clarified in a book I read, *The Top Five Regrets of the Dying: A Life Transformed by the Dearly Departing* by Bronnie Ware. It is a memoir about Bronnie's journey to self-discovery, which led her to care for the needs of the dying. Her life was transformed by the experience of tending to those who were in their final days on this earth. I admired Bronnie's honesty about her years of unfulfilling work and how she broke that mold to live the life she felt called to. The book simply retells learning to carefully follow our internal compasses.

The twelve-month break from the Silicon Valley juggernaut allowed me to experience the liberation of who I was. It was not easy; I fell a *lot*, and I still do. Yet, learning to enjoy the swim and gaining strength from the paddle back out sharpened my understanding of who I am *inside*. I learned to listen deeply to God's plan for my life. Learning to listen is a marvelous and life-changing experience that continues to evolve as I move forward today.

This newfound freedom in my identity ignited an insatiable curiosity about Heaven. I will explore this more in the next chapter, but it raised several questions for me. As a Christian, did I truly believe in the promise of paradise? What did the Bible have to say about Heaven? And what about the numerous near-death experiences (NDEs) people report? They excited my view of Heaven, but could I rely on them for guidance? How about going surfing when I got to Heaven – was that an outrageous thought, or not?

In the forthcoming section titled 5th Wave: Paradise, we embark on a quest to explore the many mysteries of Heaven. I aim to expand *your* horizons on what awaits us beyond this life. I encourage you to release preconceived notions and allow your imagination to run *wild*. Surfing in Heaven may not be as outlandish as it may sound.

Trust in the Lord with all your heart and lean not on your own understanding.
— Proverbs 3:5 (NIV)

Notes

1. Intel introduced the world's first microprocessor (a complete central processing unit on a single chip) in March 1971 (Intel 4044), which eventually led to the development of the personal computer (PC).

2. According to former world champion surfer Corky Carroll's article "Humble beginnings of surf leash" (Orange County Register, January 7, 2012).

    https://www.ocregister.com/2012/01/07/humble-beginnings-of-surf-leash/

5th Wave – Paradise

- God's promise of Heaven and the wonder that awaits us there.

18. Begin with The End in Mind

The day I die will be the best day I ever lived.
— Randy Alcorn (author of *Heaven*)

In 2021, I lost a very dear friend and running partner to a tragic mountain climbing accident. Roy Lambertson's abrupt departure left a painful void in my life. Seeing the news about the devastating accident while scanning my phone during a break at work completely stymied me. I was frozen in place, trying to contemplate this unthinkable tragedy. *It can't be.*

But it was true. Roy was gone. Our running community would never be the same without him. It was an agonizing pill for me to swallow. I sat hunched over like a stone statue for longer than I can remember as I contemplated this new reality and how to make sense of it. As Roy once told me upon hearing our dog passed at three years old, "Life is not fair." Nothing reinforced Roy's words more than *his* premature departure.

Death is a difficult topic for all of us, no matter the circumstances. Nobody wants to stare it in the face. I used to be scared to death of dying (pun intended). It was a real phobia I called "lights out," meaning life was over and nothing came after it. I remember thinking of the lights going off and never coming back on when I was alone in my bedroom as a young child at night. Death was the end of the story with no more pages to read. No memories, no nothing. Just contemplating the thought gave me the heebie-jeebies.

Becoming a Christian in my mid-thirties did not suddenly remove that fear. It wasn't as if I could just hit the delete button on my computer and remove any thought of "lights out" once I accepted Jesus into my life. It hung around for a while.

As I studied the Bible and started to pray regularly, God *slowly* began to show His presence in my life.

Over several years, light began to wash out the darkness, although it was more of a dimming effect. Understanding that death was simply a door I must go through to initiate my eternal life in Heaven became an awakening. That door was the beginning of my immortal life to come. I came to understand how the day I die *really will* be the best day of my life.

At that point, life took a dramatic turn. Heaven became a beacon of hope.

I first came across the concept of "Begin with the end in mind" in Stephen Covey's best-selling book, *7 Habits of Highly Effective People.* In Habit #2, "Begin with the End in Mind," Covey asked his readers to do a visualization exercise where they attended their own funeral and wrote the speech of four people who would speak. What do you want them to say? How would they describe you as a person? Is it in tune with how you are living now?

This storyline is an excellent self-reflection exercise I have used for my coaching clients; it can strike home like a lightning bolt to the true inner self. It prompts you to ask whether the things you write (their speeches at your funeral) reflect who you really are. A simple conversation over coffee can take on significant meaning once you consider that person speaking at your funeral. It powerfully demonstrates how you view your life and makes you rethink your priorities.

Contemplating your death can provide a reinvigorated perspective on your life.

The next question, however, is even weightier.

Suppose you *do* die. The odds are about 100 percent of that happening.

Then what?

I am planning for that to be the best day of my life. I'm going surfing. In Heaven.

Let's delve deeper into this concept. I want to start by first acknowledging that God's promise of Heaven and the wonder of what awaits us are beyond what our minds can imagine. [1] The Bible tells us God has mapped out an eternal destination that defies logic as we understand it today in our earthly, physical existence. What God has arranged is beyond us. It is a mystery for us to understand Heaven adequately. Yet, the Bible does have a *lot* to say about Heaven (over 500 mentions) and is our *only* resource for assembling a picture of what it might be like to live there. Heaven is described as a physical place where Christians will reside eternally in the presence of God after death here on Earth.

Years of study made Heaven a watershed for me. It turned the tide on how I view my death. Assimilating God's word about Heaven has given me a crystal-clear vision of where I am going when I die. Consequently, my priorities have shifted, bringing peace to the once tumultuous balance between work and life. My focus now centers on spending my remaining time on Earth preparing for the day when I can paddle out in Heaven. This life is simply a dress rehearsal, helping to lay the groundwork for that eternal ride home. I intend to ensure my surfboard is fully waxed up when I arrive.

I realize many may question the truth and accuracy of the Bible. That is okay. My journey started in the same place. Come along for the ride and hear me out. If nothing else, I am certain you will learn a thing or two along the way. Surely, you want to at least find out what the waves will be like in Heaven.

Surfing in Heaven has become a game-changer in my world. It's akin to a long tube ride that gives you a renewed perspective on your life after you exit the barrel. You become a changed individual. The back spray will lighten your load like nothing you have encountered on Earth. When you finally do kick out, the destination ahead will become unmistakably lucid.

The Birth of Surfing in Heaven

My first thoughts of *Surfing in Heaven* came to me at Lake Tahoe in the summer of 2004. Our family was attending a Mount Hermon family camp at Zephyr Cove (south shore), where the windows of our worship hall stared down onto the massive body of water encased by the snow-capped Sierra Nevada mountains. René Schlaepfer (pastor at Twin Lakes Church in Santa Cruz) led us in an engrossing five-day series on the subject of Heaven. I could not imagine a better setting for the topic.

Each day, René guided us through the scriptures on precisely what the Bible described about our eternal home in Heaven. This was my first experience hearing Heaven described as an actual *physical* place with *physical* bodies where we would spend eternity with God doing many, *if not all*, of the things we do here on Earth. He never veered off Scripture as he described a world exceeding the delight of our imagination in what it promises. René told us to let our minds run on what this new world would be like:

"Ask God to help you think accurately and inspirationally of the new Heaven and the new Earth that awaits."

As I gazed out the windows onto Lake Tahoe's brilliant, deep blue waters amidst the surrounding granite peaks, a ray of light broke through the clouds to illuminate an inspirational thought. Could there be *surfing* when I get to Heaven? My gears churned. Why not? An ocean with waves and sandy beaches seemed to fit perfectly with René's description of the physical beauty we will experience in Heaven.

I was stoked as I fantasized about what this could mean. With my eyes fixed on the light beam from above, a manifestation of heavenly surfing appeared in my head. My mind's eye saw a massive set of perfectly shaped waves rolling in at Zephyr Cove right then. Why not.

René's detailed descriptions of the new world to come allowed me to envision how surfing could very much be a part of my experience in Heaven. The perfect wave I had been searching for was coming into view. I was frantically scribbling graffiti notes into my Palm Pilot, trying to catch every word as René moved through the final book of the Bible [2], describing how Heaven will come down to reside on a "renewed" Earth as its final resting place.

Staring out over Lake Tahoe's breathtaking grandeur, it was hard to comprehend what God might do to renew what was already so magnificently beautiful. Yet the Bible clearly states God will deliver Heaven (the New Jerusalem) to a *renewed* Earth in the end. [3] My mind struggled to consider the possibilities.

Projecting that restoration onto the Earth's many bodies of water was beyond my comprehension. Surfing seemed not out of the question at all.

The more I discovered about Heaven, the more I needed to know. The week in Lake Tahoe launched a thirst for knowledge the depths of Lake Tahoe could not quench. Questions abounded in my head. What would my body be like? How big would the waves be? Will there be sand and rocks? How about sea life and plants? What temperature would the water be? Salt water or fresh water? Was a giant wave machine in Lake

Tahoe out of the question? Would I surf with my dad? The questions were endless as my mind began to paint a picture of life in eternity. What would *my* opening day in Heaven be like?

The upcoming three chapters will delve into those questions (and more) about what awaits us in Heaven.

I never had the chance to talk to Roy Lambertson about Heaven. You just didn't talk about that kind of stuff on our runs. I loved Roy. Yet, I didn't have it in me to broach the subject of his religious beliefs. I regret that now. This book is my attempt to have that discussion with my surfing friends who may not know Jesus yet. Think of it as my testimony to them. Heaven has turned the tide for me. I believe it can turn the tide in your life too.

Very truly I tell you, the one who believes has eternal life.
   — John 6:47 (NIV)

Notes

1. 1Corinthians 2:9 (TLB)

   "That is what is meant by the Scriptures which say that no mere man has ever seen, heard, or even imagined what wonderful things God has ready for those who love the Lord."

2. Revelation, chapter 21 (NIV)

3. Revelation 21:1-5 (NIV)

   "I saw the Holy City, the new Jerusalem, coming down out of Heaven from God, prepared as a bride beautifully dressed for her husband. And I heard a loud voice from the throne saying, 'Look! God's dwelling place is now among the people, and he will dwell with them. They will be his people, and God himself will be with them and be their God. He will wipe every tear from their eyes. There will be no more death or mourning or crying or pain, for the old order of things has passed away.' He who was seated on the throne said, 'I am making everything new!'"

19. Opening Day in Paradise

The serious business of heaven is joy.
— C.S. Lewis (Literary scholar and theologian)

My dear friend Phil Nicholson used to invite my son and me to join him and his son at the San Francisco 49ers' opening-day game at the now-defunct Candlestick Park. All other games of the season were second fiddle to opening day. This game was like no other.

The 49ers (and fans) went well beyond the standard football fare on opening day, signifying renewed hope for making it to another Super Bowl. Everyone was hyped to cheer the 49ers to victory. Coming here was like returning to the golf course after a long offseason break. The memories of those bad shots had been neatly sliced from your brain. A 49er loss on opening day was unthinkable. We looked forward to this game with a special appreciation for the experience to come.

The pre-game tailgate barbecues at Candlestick commenced just after daybreak and were elaborate, with everyone dressed head to toe in scarlet and gold. The 49er logo was everywhere: on cars, tables, banners, flags, chairs, ice chests, napkins, mugs, wine glasses, tattoos, clothes, and more. The atmosphere buzzed with anticipation and excitement as we fired up our Coleman barbecue, pulled the root beer off the ice for the kids, and tapped a mini keg of beer for the adults. Celebration was in the air. Wandering around the tailgate fixings was like peeking in on an open-air Octoberfest extravaganza. Amidst the savory aroma of barbecue smoke, the distant roar of the crowd inside the stadium added to the sense of anticipation, creating a surreal ambiance. The unmistakable energy of the 49er faithful enveloped the scene, setting the stage for something truly magical.

We caught our first view of the lush Bermuda grass field with spotless white lines as we plunged shoulder to shoulder into the dark cement stadium tunnel, feeling like sardines packed into a can. As the darkness turned to light, we saw the players warming up in their bleached, clean uniforms with brilliant 49er helmets reflecting the sun. It was a thing of absolute beauty. We paused to soak it in before being moved by the crowd to our seats amongst the horde of 49er faithful. The stadium music roared to the excitement of fans who were already dancing as if a touchdown had been scored.

The pre-game ceremony signaled this was not just another football game. Dignitaries were announced. The U.S. military was honored. Retired 49er players paraded onto the field. History was celebrated. Opening day was unique; it was a *new beginning.*

Opening day climaxed when US military soldiers unfurled a ginormous American flag covering the entire field as we sang our national anthem with 49er hats placed over our hearts. Four Blue Angel jets swept in for a dramatic fly-by at the climax of "the land of the free and the home of the brave." Patriotic fervor dampened my eyes as the crowd of sixty thousand cheered in praise to the booming symbolism of our freedom. The 49er players then exploded onto the field from the black tunnel with a loud cannon shot amongst a cloudburst of more fireworks and patriotic screaming. My voice was already hoarse, and the game had not even started.

Go 49ers – it's *game time*!

Opening Day in Heaven

As I anticipate my first day in Heaven, I can't help but wonder if God gives us earthly pleasures like this to provide a sampling of the experiences there. Standing in Candlestick Park and feeling the crowd's intense emotion as the Blue Angels rocketed by could be a prelude to exactly that. The Bible describes hearing the voices of hundreds of thousands of angels worshipping God in Heaven. [1] I struggle to imagine angel worship being any better than that 49ers crowd, but the Bible tells us what God has in store for us is beyond our wildest dreams. Life with God will satiate every desire we have. Our joy will be exponentially amplified. We were created for life with God. We will finally be home. I envision having my dream day in the lineup at San Onofre with good friends and family joining in. The sky is the limit, as we truly can't imagine how good it will be.

I have read more books about Heaven than I can count to satisfy my curiosity about what awaits us there. In describing Heaven, the Bible says,

"It was filled with the glory of God and flashed and glowed like a precious gem, crystal clear like jasper." [2]

Yet Heaven's real emphasis is not on Heaven's *beauty* but on the *joy* there. This joy will overwhelm us so we forget all our troubles here on Earth. In Heaven, everything will be new. [3] Earthly pleasures like the opening day festivities of the 49ers game are simply a foretaste of the heavenly joy there. As amazing as the opening day 49er game was, our "opening day" in Heaven will make the game seem like a day waiting in line at the California DMV.

Seriously.

In the Bible, Jesus Christ is the sole authority on Heaven. He is the only person in the history of humanity to have descended from Heaven to dwell on Earth and impart knowledge about its mysteries to us. Jesus had a *lot* to say about Heaven. In the book of Matthew alone, He spoke of Heaven more than any other person in the entire Bible. His message was straightforward: Fix your eyes *not* on the earthly treasures around you but on the riches in Heaven. [4] In His short three-year ministry on Earth, Jesus was like an Army recruit who had memorized the soldier's creed. He never wavered on that message.

One could argue God's purpose in sending Jesus to Earth was to tell the world about Heaven. Whether or not you believe Jesus is who He said He was (the Son of God), looking closely at what He said about Heaven is fascinating. If we narrow down to His final three days on Earth, Jesus was as clear as an ear-piercing bell on two things about Heaven.

First, Jesus said He is preparing a personalized home for us in Heaven. [5] When we finally arrive in Heaven, Jesus will have our home all built and ready for us to move in. The King James translation uses the word "*mansion*" (in my Father's house are many *mansions*). I like that picture. Jesus told the disciples He would come to take them there as soon as it was ready. Perhaps my heavenly mansion will even have an outdoor shower to rinse the sand off after a day of surfing!

When Jesus said this, He was meeting with His disciples for their *final* meal together (The Last Supper) and giving them their marching orders before His departure. In three days, He would be crucified on the cross.

To place some context around this, picture the 49er players assembled in the locker room preparing for the final game of their season. Imagine you are the head coach and have announced you are retiring after this final game. This pep talk is your last chance to address the players. What would you say to them? Surely, a strategy discussion about how to win the game is in order. You would tell them the key plays they would need to make and probably remind them this *is* your last game. Surely your speech would motivate them.

The words Jesus spoke were nothing short of astounding, considering the circumstances. The disciples would be carrying the torch forward to spread Christianity to all of Earth. Not one of the millions of Christian churches in the world today had been built yet. This was *ground zero* for Christianity. Once Jesus died, the future of Christianity rested on these 12 men.

Yet, Jesus did not use the time to review the blueprint for advancing Christianity after He was gone. Nor did he explain how they should position His departure. Instead, He left the football field entirely and simply told them He was preparing a place for them in Heaven. He gave the disciples a vision of *hope* for their future. The hope of Heaven became the foundation upon which the Christian church was built. Today, about 2.4 billion Christians in the world have staked their future on that hope. [6] In hindsight, Jesus seems to have called for a compelling play. Christianity is the largest religious group in the world.

The second noteworthy thing Jesus said during His final hours was to declare that Heaven would be *paradise*:

"Truly I tell you, today you will be with me in paradise" (Luke 23:43, NIV).

In some of the last words Jesus spoke before His death on the cross, He declared Heaven a perfect place. Jesus spoke these words to a dying thief who was hanging on a cross next to Him. As the thief accepted that Jesus was who He said He was, Jesus assured him he would be joining Him there – in *paradise*. Imagine how the thief felt to hear that from Jesus.

Jesus is crystal clear Heaven is a real, physical place, a Shangri-La compared to what we know here on Earth. A paradise for me has a connotation around surfing, with warm water, perfect waves, a white sandy beach, and, of course, palm trees full of coconuts to keep me nourished. Why not? My heavenly vision may seem outlandish, but only because we consider it from our earthly perspective. What awaits us there is beyond what we can imagine. It will be a utopia.

Jesus had the foresight to give the disciples a clear view of their future home in Heaven, providing strength to endure the difficult times ahead. The promise of paradise was the perfect motivator to get them to persevere. Amid all the muck and despair we see around us in the world today, this promise is precisely what we need as well.

The final score of the 49ers game will not matter when we get to Heaven. An opening day win is an earthly treasure. In Heaven, we will be perfect in every way: physically, morally, and in our knowledge. We will have new bodies free from the pain, death, and decay of this present world. [7] Amazingly, we *will* be the person we are today. Our memories of who we are, what we have done, and who we knew on Earth will not fade. The Bible assures us Jesus will transform our lowly bodies to be like His glorious body after the resurrection. [8] It will all be paradise in the end.

I believe God brought Jesus to Earth to tell us about our future in Heaven. He wants our lives to be filled with the joy of Heaven *today*. That deep internal joy can dissolve the work-life balance conundrum, turn the rough seas into glass, and make the deep valleys manageable when you prioritize heavenly things over earthly things. Knowing our eternal destiny gives us optimism for the future. It can only get better. Our best days are ahead of us.

I have lived long enough to realize suffering in this life is inevitable. The Bible does not claim our avoiding it once we become a Christian. In the book of John, chapter 16, verse 33 (NIV), Jesus tells His disciples "in this world you will have trouble." We will talk more about that in a later chapter, but Jesus is clear we can count on *rough water* in this life. And yet, despite our troubles, the Bible teaches all of it will be forgotten in

Heaven. This great certainty gives me the courage to face the many challenges ahead.

I can't wait to paddle out in Heaven.

But first, we must discuss why everything we do here on Earth while preparing for Heaven matters – big time.

Forever, O Lord, your Word stands firm in heaven.
   — Psalm 119:89 (TLB)

Notes

1. Revelation 5:11-12 (NIV)

   "Then I looked and heard the voice of many angels, numbering thousands upon thousands and ten thousand times ten thousand."

2. Revelation 21:10-11 (TLB)

   "In a vision he took me to a towering mountain peak, and from there I watched that wondrous city, the holy Jerusalem, descending out of the skies from God. It was filled with the glory of God and flashed and glowed like a precious gem, crystal clear like jasper."

3. Revelation 21:5 (NIV)

   "He who was seated on the throne said, 'I am making everything new!' Then he said, 'Write this down, for these words are trustworthy and true.'"

4. Matthew 6:19-21 (NIV)

   "Do not store up for yourselves treasures on Earth, where moths and vermin destroy and where thieves break in and steal. But store up for yourselves treasures in Heaven, where moths and vermin do not destroy, and where thieves do not break in and steal. For where your treasure is, there your heart will be also."

5. John 14:1-3 (TLB)

   "Let not your heart be troubled. You are trusting God, now trust in Me. There are many homes up there where my Father lives, and I am going to prepare them for your coming. When everything is ready, then I will come and get you, so that you can always be with me where I am. If this weren't so, I would tell you plainly."

6. Christianity is the world's largest religious group; in 2020, about 2.4 billion globally claim to be Christians. (https://en.wikipedia.org/wiki/Major_religious_groups)

7. Revelation 21:4 (TLB)

    "He will wipe away all tears from their eyes, and there shall be no more death, nor sorrow, nor crying, nor pain. All of that has gone forever."

8. Philippians 3:20-21 (NIV)

    "But our citizenship is in Heaven. And we eagerly await a Savior from there, the Lord Jesus Christ, who, by the power that enables Him to bring everything under His control, will transform our lowly bodies so that they will be like His glorious body."

20. Heaven Can't Wait

Kindness is the language which the deaf can hear and the blind can see.
— Mark Twain (American writer and humorist)

I first heard about Steve Jobs' death during my marketing gig at *Oracle OpenWorld* in San Francisco (October 5, 2011). It was Oracle's annual pilgrimage to shut down Howard Street, bring in the America's Cup sailboats, and paint San Francisco *Oracle* red. Our team needed a couple of iPods to award as prizes for our booth, so I escaped the madness of the Moscone Center to walk a few blocks in the warm fall daylight to the Apple store near Union Square. Amidst the evening's rush-hour swarm of pedestrians and the city's crisp autumn breeze, a fortress of candles on the sidewalk surrounding the Apple store entrance stopped me cold. Steve Jobs had just died.

Both employees and customers wandered around like zombies, ruminating over the shocking news. It was as if the store needed to cease operations and digest the depth of it all. I also found myself in a state of denial. The suddenness of his passing hit hard. Merely a day before, the excitement of the iPhone 4s unveiling had filled the air, drawing crowds of tech enthusiasts like bees to honey, eager to taste Apple's latest creation. And yet the incongruity was the architect of it all had vanished. No one could quite grasp it.

Steve Jobs was an iconic figure in the computer industry, known for his visionary leadership and relentless pursuit of perfection. His revolutionary products transformed entire industries. Suddenly, he was gone at the premature age of 56. His passing was a sonic boom throughout Silicon Valley. His departure left a void impossible to fill. We all had to rethink our world without Steve Jobs.

Walter Isaacson's enthralling biography, *Steve Jobs,* was released just a few weeks later. As I immersed myself in Isaacson's portrayal of Jobs' life, I could not put the book down. Born only a month apart from Jobs, I was keen to explore his story and gain insight into his remarkable genius. In the words of Isaacson, Jobs was the "ultimate icon of inventiveness and applied imagination."[1] He combined artistic creativity with technological innovation to revolutionize the computer industry.

Steve Jobs was known to "think differently." His inventions completely transformed computer design and the user interface. To place his impact into a surfing context would be to compare him to Bob Simmons's influence on lightweight surfboard design in the 1940s. [2] Simmons was the first to introduce lightweight foam and fiberglass into surfboard design. Before that, everyone was riding 100-pound redwood planks. Nobody then could have predicted the shortboard revolution following Simmons' ingenuity. Surfing was changed forever.

I was fascinated with how Steve Jobs' career paralleled the explosive growth of Silicon Valley following the invention of the personal computer (PC). The story of his emergence from the Los Altos garage to being the co-founder of Apple Computers was like reading a Stephen Ambrose war epic on how Silicon Valley was won. Even his high school days captivated me, including the pranks he orchestrated. (I could relate.) Yet, for all those days I spent surfing in high school, Steve was fiddling with computers in his garage, preparing to change the world.

As I devoured Isaacson's narrative, an element of Steve Jobs' personality made me uncomfortable and deeply stirred my concern for who he was at the core. At times, Jobs could be a sociopathic monster in handling people who seemed to get in the way of where he was trying to go. His unruly antics were well-documented. Some stories of him thrashing his people who did not deliver on his expectations were horrific. Most would agree he reached the top of the mountain at an agonizing price to many who worked alongside him. The book was a fascinating character study.

Yet, his list of accomplishments is unequaled. A short list of new product introductions in 30 years at Apple speaks to his genius:

- Apple I, 1976 (Apple II, 1977)

- Macintosh, 1984

- iMac, 1998

- iPod, 2001

- iTunes, 2003

- iPhone, 2007

- iPad, 2010

Despite all this, as I read Isaacson's account, I could not help but wonder: Was it worth it? At what price did Steve Jobs attain this level of notoriety? How might God judge him? Small Fry, Lisa Brennan-Jobs' memoir, details her upbringing as Jobs' first child and sheds light on the repercussions of his behavior. Despite his reluctance to acknowledge her as his daughter, her perspective offered a poignant glimpse into the challenges of growing up as an inconvenience to her success-obsessed father. Witnessing Jobs' stardom through a child's lens was thought-provoking and unsettling.

As Apple became the world's first company to record a market capitalization of $1 trillion in 2018, much of the credit surely goes to Steve Jobs. According to our world's definition of success, he *did* come out on top. Steve Jobs experienced acclaim beyond what anyone could have imagined in his quest to deliver products that changed the world. By worldly standards, he won.

I would like to propose another side to that coin. What if we evaluate a person's life with a different standard? What if everything we do here on planet Earth has an *eternal* value? Would that change the way we all view our lives today? Would that change our view of Steve Jobs?

Everything We Do in This Life Matters

There is an urgent message in the Bible many Christians miss. Jesus told us everything we do in this life matters once we reach Heaven. As good as we know Heaven will be, one significant point is missing: Heaven does not begin when you die – it begins right now, *today*. To put it in Silicon Valley vernacular, it is happening in *real-time* as you read this. Heaven can't wait.

This is a momentous point if you aim to build a life of enduring significance. I lived most of my life without truly grasping it. Having a vision of my future in Heaven has helped me rearrange my priorities and clarify my identity. Eternity is motivating me to take this life very seriously.

There is a spiritual battle in our world today where eternal issues are at stake. The temptation of the evil one is to lure us into complacency to think how we live this life does not matter. Such thinking is a lie – don't believe it. What happens in Las Vegas does not truly stay in Las Vegas.

Every day we live on Earth impacts our life in Heaven forever. The person I am becoming today is preparing me for the person I shall be for eternity. Playing Maximus in the movie *Gladiator*, Russell Crowe summed it up nicely:

"What you do in this life echoes through eternity."

According to research, we can spend up to 90,000 hours at work in our lifetime. [3] In Silicon Valley, this estimate is grossly conservative based on a 40-hour work week (ha ha). Does it matter how we spend that time? The race I had been running was to do whatever it took in those 90,000 hours to maximize my income so I could hopefully cash out early and start enjoying life. The winners were the ones who crossed the line first.

Jesus had a different take. He made it clear there is a direct connection between what I chose to do in those 90,000 hours and the life I will spend in paradise. It is not about maximizing my earthly treasures; it is about building a future for my heavenly treasures.

"For the Son of Man is going to come in His Father's glory with his angels, and then He will reward each person according to what they have done" (Matthew 16:27, NIV).

When we reach Heaven, Jesus tells us we will be repaid according to how we have lived on Earth. Even though we are in Heaven, and our joy is complete, we will have rewards waiting for us when we arrive. This promise is not an isolated incident in the Bible. There are *many* examples of Jesus telling us what we do here on Earth really matters once we get to Heaven. This concept is a recurring theme in the New Testament:

- "Yes, leap for joy! For **you will have a great reward awaiting you** in Heaven" (Luke 6:23, TLB).

- "If you want to be perfect, go and sell everything you have and give the money to the poor, and **you will have treasure in Heaven**" (Matthew 19:21, TLB).

- "Be very glad! for **a tremendous reward awaits you** up in Heaven" (Matthew 5:12, TLB).

Statements like "leap for joy" and "be very glad" are indicators this topic gets special attention from God. He is keeping track of us as we live our lives here on Earth. Eventually (when we cross over into Heaven), He will reward us for how well we've done.

I must clarify this is *not* about doing good works on Earth to *get* to Heaven. The Bible states going to Heaven is strictly an act of *faith* – not an act of *works*. It is a free gift from God requiring only your belief. The Apostle Paul makes this point quite clearly in his letter to the Ephesians in the New Testament.

"God saved you by his grace when you believed. And you can't take credit for this; it is a gift from God. Salvation is not a reward for the good things we have done, so none of us can boast about it" (Ephesians 2:8-9, NLT).

One of the more renowned verses in the Bible states this quite clearly:

"For this is how God loved the world: He gave his one and only Son, so that everyone who believes in him will not perish but have eternal life" (John 3:16, NLT).

It is important to note this discussion is not about winners and losers. If we are already in Heaven, *everyone* will be a winner. But Jesus is clear there will be recompense waiting when we get there. Several books have been written on this topic. One of my favorites is Bruce Wilkinson's *A Life God Rewards: Why Everything You Do Today Matters Forever,* which hits it head-on.

Wilkinson explains this concept of rewards by separating our beliefs (faith) from our behaviors (actions). Our *beliefs* are what unlock the door to our eternal life in Heaven. If we believe Jesus is who He said He is (the son of God), we will go to Heaven. That is what Wilkinson calls having *faith.* No amount of hard work can ever earn God's favor. He is the One who has done the work God requires for our salvation: Jesus died on the cross as our substitute to pay the penalty for our sins. He is the pioneer and perfecter of our faith.

However, our *behaviors* unlock the door to rewards and determine how we will spend eternity. Our behavior on Earth will impact the rewards we receive when we get to Heaven. Jesus promised generous rewards for our behaviors here on Earth. Following are just a few Bible references as examples of how these rewards could be earned while we live our lives here on Earth:

- God sees and rewards good deeds (Ephesians 6:8)

- God rewards those who deny themselves (Matthew 16:24)

- God rewards those who show compassion to the needy (Luke 14:13)

- God rewards those who treat their enemies kindly (Luke 6:35)

- God rewards those who trust Him to endure difficult circumstances (Hebrews 10:34)

- God rewards those who live faithfully (1 Corinthians 4:2-5)

- God rewards those who persevere under persecution (Luke 6:22-23)

- God richly rewards a life of godliness (2Peter 3:11-14)

- God rewards those who make wise use of their resources and opportunities (Hebrews 11:26)

And I should add these rewards are forever. Looking at how fast my life here on Earth has flown by has my attention. God is telling us our life here will impact our life there, forever!

So, what will these rewards in Heaven be? What might they look like?

The Greek root of *rewards* is *misthos,* which translates to "wages." Jesus appears to be telling us we will get paid for our time here on Earth and it will have unending value in Heaven. And He is the one who will sign the check.

Despite my studies in this area, I am far from speculating what those heavenly rewards could mean. Knowing what I do about Jesus, I feel confident they will be specific to each person and well worth the effort. I like the view American Pastor John MacArthur Jr. has on it:

"There will be varying degrees of reward in Heaven. That shouldn't surprise us: There are varying degrees of giftedness even here on Earth."

Following are a few comments from Christian leaders on these eternal rewards:

- ### Charles R. Swindoll:
". . . He promises a reward. And we can be sure He will keep His promise."

- ### Jonathan Edwards:
"There are many mansions in God's house because Heaven is intended for various degrees of honor and blessedness."

- ### Charles H. Spurgeon:
"Seek secrecy for your good deeds."

- ### Theodore H. Epp:
"God is eager to reward us and does everything possible to help us lay up rewards."

- ### John Wesley:
"God will reward everyone according to his works."

- ### R.C. Sproul:
"If a person has been faithful in many things through many years, then he will be acknowledged by His Master, who will say to him, "Well done, thou good and faithful servant... there are at least 25 occasions where the New Testament clearly teaches that we will be granted rewards according to our works."

- ### Billy Graham:
". . . and the work we have done must stand the ultimate test; final exams come at the Judgment Seat of Christ when we receive our rewards."

- **Martin Luther:**
  "Therefore, he who does good works and guards himself
  against sin, God will reward."

Jesus made it very clear. He came to tell us about Heaven and once
we get there, it gets even better. When people asked him how to get to
Heaven, he boiled it down to one word: *love*. [4] It seems so simple. Yet,
it is precisely what the world needs a lot more of today.

These words challenge our lifestyle here in Silicon Valley (and
beyond). In surfing terminology, we must learn to paddle against the
current. When I am out at Steamer Lane on a big northwest winter swell,
the constant push of powerful waves toward shore requires strong,
consistent paddling to maintain my position in the lineup. Everything
around me is going the other way.

Going against the current is how Jesus wants us to live our life here
on Earth. Our faith will get us to Heaven, but those powerful paddling
skills to maintain our position in the lineup will reap the rewards. This
discussion of rewards is having an impact on me *now*. My life is in the
fourth quarter here on Earth. As I look ahead to Heaven, discovering a
secluded surfing spot with warm water and flawless waves doesn't seem
so unbelievable. Why not?

In the final few paragraphs of Isaacson's book (Chapter 42, Legacy:
The Brightest Heaven of Invention), Steve Jobs reflected on his death,

> "I'm about fifty-fifty on believing in God. For most of
> my life, I've felt there must be more to our existence than
> meets the eye. But on the other hand, perhaps it's like an
> on-off switch. Click! And you're gone. Maybe that's why
> I never liked to put on-off switches on Apple devices."

Our life truly is a mist that appears briefly and then quickly fades. [5]
I want God to be proud of the life I lived here on Earth. There will be
no penalties – we will be in Heaven. Yet, the work each of us is doing in
our life here on Earth helps construct the mansion God builds for us
there. Nothing is ever lost or wasted with God. Everything we do on
Earth will build on our everlasting life in Heaven. Every day really does
matter.

In his book *The Treasure Principle* [6], Randy Alcorn frames this point with a picture of a dot connected to a line:

A dot represents your entire life history on planet Earth, and a continuous line with no end represents your eternal life in Heaven. So, the question to ask yourself is whether you are living for the dot or the line.

I must admit I have lived mostly for the dot. It's a ton of work to paddle against those currents when the world is going the other way. It's as if the world is upside down, and I am in a constant battle to stay aligned with the instruction Jesus gives us:

"What good will it be for someone to gain the whole world, yet forfeit their soul?" (Matthew 16:26, NIV).

Steve Jobs built an empire that left him on top of the mountain in Silicon Valley. It is hard to argue with the success he achieved. He maximized the dot. You might even think of the $5 billion Apple campus in Cupertino (aka "the spaceship") as an iconic symbol of maximizing the dot (2.8 million square feet of floor space and 1 mile in circumference). It is even said to be visible from outer space.

And yet, Jesus came into this world to redefine true greatness. In His kingdom, the least are seen as the greatest. The meek inherit the Earth. The servant outshines the ruler. The first ends up last, and the last is first. [7] Jesus tells us to focus on the line with no end. Those treasures will last for eternity.

Heaven can't wait. It is happening right now.

Look, I am coming soon! My reward is with me, and I will give to each person according to what they have done.

— Revelation 22:12 (NIV)

Notes

1. Isaacson, Walter. *Steve Jobs*. New York: Simon and Schuster: 2011.

2. Bob Simmons was the "mad scientist" who pioneered lightweight surfboard design in the 1940s in southern California and is often credited as the father of the modern surfboard. As a Cal Tech graduate who worked as a mathematician at Douglas Aircraft, he radically changed surfboard design more than anyone else before or since him. As stated on the Surfing Heritage & Culture Center website, "Bob Simmons was the first person to consciously and purposefully apply hydrodynamic theory to create dynamic lift in surfboards; the first one to use fiberglass and resin to strengthen lighter weight boards; and the first one to define a surfboard and describe how it works." Tragically, Simmons died while surfing Windansea Beach in Lo Jolla on a big surf day in 1954 at the age of 35.

   https://en.wikipedia.org/wiki/Bob_Simmons_(surfer)

3. Gettysburg College study: One third of your life is spent at work.

   https://www.gettysburg.edu/news/stories?id=79db7b34-630c-4f49-ad32-4ab9ea48e72b

4. Mark 12:28-31 (TLB)

   "…The Lord our God is the one and only God. And you must love Him with all your heart and soul and mind and strength. The second is: 'You must love others as much as yourself.' No other commandments are greater than these."

5. James 4:14 (NIV)

   "Why, you do not even know what will happen tomorrow. What is your life? You are a mist that appears for a little while and then vanishes."

6. Alcorn, Randy. *The Treasure Principle: Unlocking The Secrets Of Joyful Giving.* Colorado Spring, CO: Penguin Random Books, LLC, 2001.

7. Luke 13:30; Mark 10:31; Matthew 27:64; Matthew 20:16 (all NIV)

21. Tides of Evidence

I can see how it might be possible for a man to look down upon the Earth and be an atheist, but I cannot conceive how a man could look up into the Heavens and say there is no God.
— Abraham Lincoln (16th president of the United States)

One of my favorite parts of our many trips to Baja in the 1970s and 1980s was spending an entire day on the beach, watching the ebb and flow of the tide. There is nothing like it for absolute rest and slowing down. San Felipe, Mexico is one of the more glorious spots for this leisurely activity. It has one of the most significant tidal flows in the world, which can expose up to a kilometer of bare sand at low tide due in part to the Colorado River delta to the north.

We would take our beach chairs out to the water's edge at the bottom of the low tide and then sit and soak in the warm Baja sun as the ripples of the incoming tide slowly crept back in. The goal was to test the elements of nature to see how long we could stay seated in our beach chairs until the incoming waves finally pushed us over. Of course, plenty of cold beer helped us stay appropriately hydrated amid this taxing ordeal.

Monitoring the incoming tide in San Felipe with Steve Schott (right)
- circa 1988

For most of my life, I have studied the tides at my favorite surf spots in search of epic waves to ride. Aside from the size of the incoming swell, nothing impacts the quality of the surf as much as the tide. The tidal charts (or tide tables), akin to a surfer's indispensable compass, serve as our guiding light in the pursuit of optimal waves.

To briefly explain, four distinct tidal movements occur within each twenty-four-hour period, manifesting as two high tides and two low tides, courtesy of Earth's rotation. These four tidal conditions can have a profound impact on the quality of the surf. For example, in winter, Steamer Lane (Santa Cruz) is often best when the tide is coming back in following a "low" tide. It is even better if that incoming tide follows a "minus" low tide when the low tide dips below 0.0 feet (like the example below at 8:27 am, -0.4 ft.).

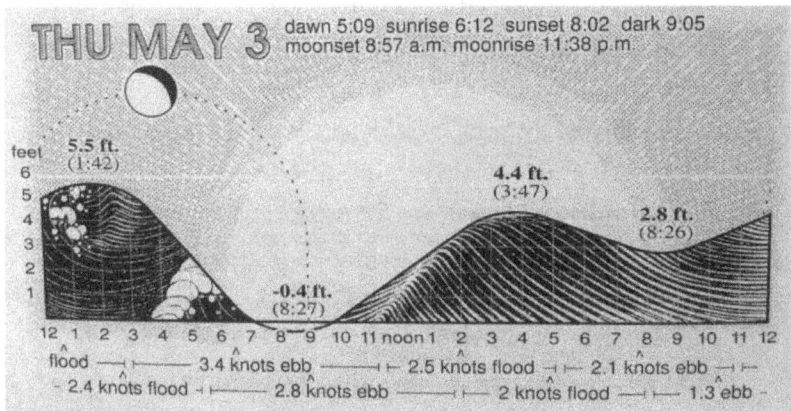

The tidal chart for surfers

However, at San Onofre (San Clemente), the best surf is all about the south swells that sweep up the coast in the summer at high tide. Classic San Onofre peaks roll in at Old Man's, allowing you to go left or right on that high tide's incoming or outgoing side (from 2 pm to 6 pm above).

One of the innumerable examples God bestowed upon us to authenticate the wonder of His creation is the daily rhythm of our tides. Contemplating how this rhythm works is astonishing. The tides are far from random and testify to the absolute brilliance of God's design.

Because two-thirds of our planet is covered in water, the gravitational interplay between Earth and the moon produce the ebb and flow of our tides. However, this becomes insanely complex when considering factors like planetary rotation, gravitational forces, the pull of the sun, the effects of weather, and the intricate choreography of tidal patterns encircling our seven continents.

Our moon offers compelling evidence of an intelligent designer. Earth stands alone in our solar system as the sole possessor of a solitary moon, which happens to be disproportionately large relative to our planet's size. Positioned just right in size and distance, our moon, in tandem with the sun, orchestrates the symphony of tidal movements essential for life on Earth.

Eric Metaxes sums it up well in his book *Miracles*:

> The moon's considerable gravity gives our oceans their ebbing and flowing tides. If the moon were slightly bigger, it would cause our tides to be much more extreme since a larger moon would exert that much more gravitational pull. With one-hundred-foot tides, there could be no coastal cities or towns or villages. If the moon were slightly smaller and had less gravitational pull, the tides would be insufficient to cleanse coastal seawater and replenish its nutrients. If the moon were any size other than its size, life as we know it wouldn't exist. [1]

As Abraham Lincoln acknowledged, it all points a finger to God. Our moon truly is a miracle.

Evidence of Heaven

If you ask a Christian to provide evidence beyond the tides of God's existence (and, thereby, Heaven), they will likely point you to Jesus and the miraculous powers He demonstrated in His brief life on Earth. The substantiation of His resurrection from the dead could be included. They might also argue the Old Testament prophets told of His coming hundreds of years before His birth. They could even point to the proof of lives they witnessed Jesus dramatically change, the most powerful witness of all. I've got a friend whose life has been transformed by getting to know who Jesus is. He went from jail to Jesus and has never looked back.

I want to address a different kind of evidence that does not get much attention in Christian circles. Many published books are available today about people who claim to have experienced a journey to Heaven and back, possibly offering a glimpse of what God has in store for us. There are also several books on people experiencing hell, but I don't plan to go down that path.

Clearly, we are stepping outside the Bible by looking at these stories. I have read many of the books published on this subject. [2] Some I have read multiple times. A few popular books have been released as major motion pictures. There are several of these books I *don't* recommend. Only God can truly judge the authenticity of what people have written about Heaven.

I view these stories as fiction, like reading a novel where you can explore what might be possible. In each one, the author is adamant they *did* catch a glimpse of Heaven. There is no way to authenticate their experiences, although many do not stray far from what Scripture says about Heaven. They all speak to a world beyond our most incredulous thoughts of what Heaven might be like. In almost every story, the author felt such an overwhelming sense of love, peace, and joy (and more) in Heaven that they did not want to return to their earthly home. What they experienced was far more significant. They *were* home, and they wanted to stay there.

I want to review a couple of these stories to open our eyes to what might be possible. Let your imagination run with this. The point is to envision what eternity *might* be like.

Each story fascinated me with descriptions of experiences the author had and how it impacted the life they now live on Earth. All of them were dramatically changed because of their experience. It was as if they were allowed to see "the end" and start over with a renewed perspective. The experience turned their bucket lists upside down. Reading each personal account has changed *me*. Why these experiences happen to a select few is God's mystery. But I don't think we can ignore the stories they tell.

90 Minutes in Heaven [3] was the first book (also a movie) I stumbled across during a family vacation. It is the story of Don Piper, a Texas pastor, who died in a horrific car crash on January 18, 1989. Paramedics arrived on the scene, found no pulse, and declared him dead. Piper wrote a powerful account of the next 90 minutes he spent in Heaven before returning to Earth.

His description of Heaven impacted me so profoundly I immediately had my wife Marla and our two kids read it while we were all together on vacation. It was the first time I had read anything about the experience in Heaven with such incredible detail. It gave me goosebumps as the author described a *"welcoming party"* of people he had known and loved on Earth, including his grandfather, great-grandmother, and high school classmates.

Piper admitted words could not do justice to the experience. Years passed before he spoke in public about it. In his words, *"I considered it a sacred secret."*

His story sparked a desire in me to find more. I found it fascinating and encouraging to read stories of people whose experiences changed them forever. They all spoke about experiencing a love far exceeding anything they had ever known. They seemed to taste the truth of their real purpose in life.

Night Dive To Heaven [4] by Ian McCormack is particularly of interest to me as Ian is a surfer who was living the dream of my youth by traveling the world with his best friend in search of the perfect wave. His endless summer sojourn takes a life-altering turn when he is pronounced dead in a hospital on the island of Mauritius (off East Africa) following multiple stings from a box jellyfish, renowned as one of nature's deadliest creatures. Ian was a self-professed atheist at the time who had never read the Bible, yet his remarkable journey of returning to life forever changed by his encounter with Jesus Christ is one not to miss. In *The Perfect Wave*, a 2014 film depicting Ian's story (on Amazon Prime), his view of Heaven was familiar to other narratives I have read, and not in any way contradictory to what the Bible tells us. Ian's experience transformed him. He became an ordained pastor who spends his life bearing testimony worldwide (over 75 million people to date) about the truth of what the Bible tells us about Heaven. In his words:

> ... my eyes met a fresh new world. Green pastures and lush orchards under blue skies thrilled the farm boy in me. A crystal-clear river wound through a deep-green forest, and upon this living tapestry, the Creator had embroidered colorful flowers. In the distance, a succession of endless mountains kindled my desire to see what lay beyond them.

Following his encounter with Heaven, Ian spent the next forty-two years telling people about the truth of the Bible. The comparisons to the life of the apostle Paul (Saul of Tarsus), who wrote so much of the New Testament, are unavoidable. I was so captivated with Ian's story that I reached out to interview him on my blog [(4)]. And just in case you are wondering, yes, I did ask Ian if there would be surfing in Heaven. You are going to like his answer.

My favorite book, which reads more like poetry about Heaven, is *Intra Muros* [(5)], written by Rebecca Springer in 1898. Rebecca described a unique atmosphere of life in Heaven like no other book I have come across. Published 120 years ago, Springer writes of an experience she had of going to Heaven while seriously ill in a Kentville, Illinois care home.

The author describes her experiences over an extensive period before her return. She never quantifies how long she was there, but I would liken it to 90 *days* in Heaven rather than 90 *minutes*. Rebecca describes her inability to chronicle the depth and wonder of the experience:

> I am painfully aware of the fact that I can never paint for others the scenes as they appeared to me during those wonderful days. If I can only dimly show the close linking of the two lives – the mortal with the divine – as they then appeared to me, I may be able to partly tear the veil from the death we so dread and show it to be only an open door into a new and beautiful phase of the life we now live.

Her description of immersion in a body of water in Heaven was incredibly captivating. Finally, I had an account of people getting *wet* in Heaven. Rebecca constructed an inconceivable image of what it would be like to experience heavenly water and waves. Here is one excerpt where she describes the movement of the waves.

"... as they came and went in ceaseless motion, caught up this sparkling sand and carried it on their crests, like the phosphorescence we sometimes see in the wake of a vessel in mid-ocean."

Her detailed description of swimming boggled my mind as I imagined how surfing in Heaven could go well beyond what my imagination could fabricate. She described the water "in both temperature and density, [as] almost identical with the air." When going under the water, she quickly realized with a laugh that nothing had changed.

"I could not only breathe, but laugh and talk, see and hear, as naturally under the water as above it."

Best of all, there is no toweling off after exiting the water.

". . . the moment the air struck my face and hair, I realized that I would need no towel or brush. My flesh, my hair, and even my beautiful garments, were soft and dry as before the water touched them."

This book sits on my bedstand, and I often read a page at night to let the words sink into my soul before falling asleep. It is a treasure.

Not all these books are written by Christian authors. I find it even more arresting to hear people voice their experiences without including knowledge of the Bible. *Proof of Heaven: A Neurosurgeon's Journey into the Afterlife* [6] is one example. Eben Alexander, a Jewish faculty member at Harvard Medical School, writes about his near-death experience in a meningitis-induced coma for seven days in 2008. He was so enthralled by the incident he used his vast experience as a neurosurgeon to scientifically prove his experience could not possibly have been a dream.

Alexander embarked on a quest to validate his experience over those seven days as more than a mere fabrication of the brain. He concluded ". . . the death of the body and the brain are not the end of consciousness; the human experience continues beyond the grave." Alexander claimed the place he went to was so real it made the life we are living here on Earth like a dream in comparison.

"When Will the Heaven Begin?"

While vacationing in Portland, Oregon, our family dedicated most of a day to exploring Powell's bookstore, renowned as the largest independent bookstore in the world. At Powell's, you can pick your favorite subject and easily lose an entire day going through the section, including many books not available online. After doing my due diligence in the "surfing" section, I wandered over to a section on "Heaven" and was overwhelmed by the books.

I soon was engrossed in a book I could not put down: *When Will the Heaven Begin?: This Is Ben Breedlove's Story* by Ally Breedlove. [7] In this gripping narrative, Ally recounts the life of her older brother, Ben Breedlove, who grappled with a congenital heart condition that shadowed him from birth. Tragically, Ben's life came to an end at the age of 18, on Christmas evening, following a day filled with profound family joy. Yet, despite his physical struggles, Ben harbored an unwavering certainty about his destination in Heaven.

In this book, Ally speaks to a video Ben had posted on YouTube to chronicle his attraction to Heaven. I gathered my family to watch the video in stunned amazement on the cold cement floor in Powell's. Ben tells his story with flip cards about how he had been waiting for Heaven to begin. Ben experienced cardiac arrest on four separate occasions and sampled Heaven's Perfect Peace.

Ally discovered the video while rummaging through his stuff on Christmas night after his passing. Ben's story is one to behold, no matter your beliefs about Heaven. As a vibrant eighteen-year-old boy with a full and active life, including a girlfriend and loving family, Ben realized what awaited him in Heaven was far better than his life here on Earth. He left the video to comfort his family when God took him home. Search for "This is my story (Part 1)" on YouTube to locate it. At the time of this writing, it has over nine million views.

These stories paint a striking and consistent picture of Heaven as a physical place of indescribable beauty where our bodies are transformed into perfect selves. Any suffering we experience here, no matter how intense, is ultimately canceled out by the love awaiting us in Heaven. Those who have tasted it say they no longer fear death – they would rather be there than here.

Interestingly, each person's experience of Heaven seems to be different, as if God had individually prepared a place for each of them. [8] They all pondered why God had chosen them to have the experience and what to do with it after returning to life on Earth. Most of these authors believe God gave them these experiences to spread the joy and hope for what awaits us in Heaven.

For those who have trusted God, an amazing new place awaits us. As I continued along my path in Silicon Valley, Roger Williams' words of wisdom at Mount Hermon Family Camp on Lake Tahoe echoed in my heart about changing the way I live today – for Heaven:

"It's not the end – it's . . . the beginning!"

I have lived long enough to realize suffering in this life is inevitable. There is no avoiding it. Yet, despite our troubles, the Bible teaches all of it will be forgotten in Heaven.

"There will be no more death or sorrow or crying or pain. All these things are gone forever" (Revelation 21:3-5).

Having this great certainty gives me the courage to face the valleys ahead. Ben Breedlove had his share of valleys with his heart condition. Seeing a glimpse of what awaited him gave him the conviction to tell the world he was ready to go, even though he was 18 years old and had his whole life on Earth before him. He knew what was coming would far outweigh this earthly life.

Thinking about Heaven *now* will dramatically impact our lives here on Earth. Heaven should be our first and most important priority. It is urgent. We are built for it – it is God's plan for our lives. Staying focused on Heaven can transform our life here on Earth. To think otherwise is to take a very short-term view of our existence.

This next section, "6th Wave: Rock Dance," transitions from a discussion of the heavenly realm to the here and now in my story. It presents an abrupt change in focus, mirroring the unpredictability of life itself. Whether or not you are a believer in the promise of Heaven, we *all* have our ups and downs. Drawing upon surfing imagery, I liken this to a precarious rock dance at a minus low tide, when one must carefully navigate through the rocks to get back to shore. Anyone who has been there will tell you it is not easy, especially in the 1960s, when we did it with bare feet. To this day, I remember my dad's bloodied feet the time he carried me into the beach at San Onofre on a very low tide day.

The kingdom of heaven is like a merchant looking for fine pearls. When he found one of great value, he went away and sold everything he had and bought it.
 — Matthew 13:45–46 (NIV)

Notes

1. Metaxas, Eric. *Miracles: What They Are, Why They Happen, and How They Can Change Your Life*. New York: Dutton, 2014.

2. If you want a list of books I recommend on Heaven, go to: www.SurfingForBalance.com/resources.

3. Piper, Don. *90 Minutes in Heaven: A True Story of Death & Life*. Grand Rapids, MI: Revell, 2004.

4. McCormack, Ian (as told to Richard Drebert). *Night Dive To Heaven*. 2023.

   My interview with Ian McCormack can be found at: www.SurfingForBalance.com/resources

5. Springer, Rebecca. *Intra Muros: My Dream of Heaven*. 1898.

6. Alexander, Eben. *Proof of Heaven: A Neurosurgeon's Journey into the Afterlife*. New York: Simon & Schuster, 2012.

7. Breedlove, Ally. *When Will the Heaven Begin?: This Is Ben Breedlove's Story*. New York: Dutton, 2013.

8. John 14:2-3 (KJV)

   "In my Father's house are many mansions: if it were not so, I would have told you. I go to prepare a place for you. And if I go and prepare a place for you, I will come again, and receive you unto myself; that where I am, there ye may be also."

6th Wave – Rock Dance

- Learning to dance through life.

22. "A Lotta Shit . . ."

Age is an issue of mind over matter. If you don't mind, it doesn't matter.
— Mark Twain

While this newfound knowledge of Heaven was having a dramatic and very positive impact on my spiritual life, I was also discovering new challenges with my physical body since I passed the mid-century point in age. Sometimes, pain was involved, and I had to learn how to delicately navigate my way forward. On good days, it could be like learning a new dance step. On bad days, I would just grin and bear it, knowing that this, too, will pass.

I was beginning to feel like my 1970s vintage Infinity surfboard, which now requires a little extra resin and fiberglass between surf sessions to keep it going. The white foam is now a faded brown, and the smooth fiberglass deck has plenty of dents and dings, which I have repaired over the years. It still rides fine, but it does take more nurturing to stay afloat after all those years of surfing.

This pattern of physical breakdowns showed up most notably in my running career. Don't get me wrong, I am strictly a recreational runner. But I *love* running, especially longer distances. Running is a part of who I am. With all the miles I have pounded out over the years running marathons, ultra-marathons, and triathlons, I must confess my body began to show some wear and tear once I hit my fifties. These days, I know how to doctor things up with a bit of resin and fiberglass (and DMSO) to keep going, but I'd be lying to say those miles don't hurt my body more than they used to. I'm a lot smarter about preparing, and I focus on just getting to the starting line and letting the rest take care of itself. As they say, "If you don't mind, it doesn't matter."

In 2007, a half marathon unfolded an almost prophetic story.

Big Sur Half Marathon

On a seasonably crisp October morning in Monterey, I was approaching mile 11 in the Big Sur Half Marathon when my view on life after 50 took a jolt. Big Sur is a relatively fast half marathon for time (it does not have hills, as its name might imply), and it is incredibly well-organized for a race of its size (~5,000 runners).

I had run a *hard* first ten miles and was struggling to regain my focus for the final three while ignoring the red flares my body was sending me to slow down. I had turned 50 earlier in the year and was intent on proving I could still run a fast time. Ha.

Oblivious to the serene setting of sailboats moored in quiet coves as we ran along the bike trail in Pacific Grove, I pulled up to a tall and lanky runner who had been in my sights for a couple of miles. He was running hard, so I latched on to his side to keep pace and regain some composure for a strong finish. My time goal was in sight, and I figured this guy could help pull me in. We had covered a half mile or so side-by-side when he suddenly blurted out to me:

"How old are you?"

Wait, what? I'm struggling for oxygen, and this guy asks me my age?

This was not a time to be conversing. We were both breathing hard and near the end of our ropes. If I had the grit to initiate anything (and I didn't), I might have babbled out a one-way, "good job" or "hang tough."

"How old are you?" just hit me wrong.

As we bumped shoulders coming off the bike trail onto the street at Cannery Row for a long stretch of open pavement, I glanced at him. He appeared to be sizing me up. Did he think I was a threat in his age division?

Finally, I found it in myself to respond, mostly out of the angst of having to say *anything* at this point of the race:

"Fifty! How old are YOU?"

"Fifty-nine," was his immediate reply as we both continued to push the pace on the open street. I was glimpsing the finish line banner less than a mile ahead and decided to put on a final kick to get in. As he slowly faded behind me, I was hit with a verbal cannon shot:

"A lotta shit between 50 and 59!"

Say what?

The purpose and conviction in the words rattled me. I found myself in a dither as I crossed the finish line, suddenly oblivious of the time I had worked so hard for. Why the heck did he have to say that, and what on earth did he mean?

With the masses of sweaty bodies, I stumbled through the finishing chute looking like a lost soldier who had just been hit by mortar fire. As I claimed my platter of free food, none of which looked appealing, I scanned around to confront him. He had vanished, and I never saw him again.

I mentioned the exchange to my fellow warriors at the finish line party, and we all laughed as we guzzled down our hard-earned post-race rewards while listening to the rock band powered by people riding exercise bicycles. Big Sur always has a fantastic finish-line party, and we were, of course, oblivious to the road that lay ahead.

Fast-forward nine years to age 59, I knew *exactly* what he meant.

"A lotta shit . . ." just about sums it up. Mine started with knee pain and progressed from there to my back going out on the day before I had signed up to run an ultra-marathon. I recovered from that to encounter rotator cuff surgery, which I wouldn't wish upon my worst enemy. The list goes on.

This encounter has become legendary among my running community as we kid each other about the various ailments we experience while pushing our bodies to untold extremes in various sporting escapades. The running joke (pun intended) when one of us is injured is to say:

"Well, you know, *'A lotta shit!'*"

In this world you will have trouble. But take heart! I have overcome the world.
— John 16:33 (NIV)

23. Stop and Smell the Roses

Those who hope in me will not be disappointed.
— Isaiah 49:23 (NIV)

We planted a red rose bush in our front yard when my dear mom passed away in January 2007. Anyone who knew Char was aware of her passion for the color red. That rose bush has been in full bloom on her birthday every year since. It has been a remarkable reminder to me of her spirit. Yet often, I would zip in or out of our driveway in the car, too hurried to take notice of the latest blossom, let alone pause for a few seconds to savor the fragrant aroma. I was too stressed out and in a hurry.

Stressing Out

Growing up in Corona del Mar in the 1960s, I don't think the word "stress" was in my vocabulary. Don't get me wrong; I had my challenges. It was mostly around money. Our family never seemed to have much. My parents grew up during the Depression and knew how to get by on almost nothing. Dad was especially good at this. Since Mom didn't drive, Dad had control of the grocery shopping. I remember my grandmother (mom's side) visiting from Utah and exclaiming there was no food in the house. She would immediately go out on a shopping spree to get provisions to fill the cupboards and refrigerator.

Today, my kids are under different kinds of stress. They tell me stress is in their DNA. It is unavoidable. I get stressed just thinking about their stress. I think we *all* would agree stress is a byproduct of living in today's world. So much seems to be out of whack. In surfing terms, life can be gnarly. Sometimes, I feel like I am in a constant rock dance without any hope of reaching the sand. I just keep hopping from rock to rock in hope of a soft landing.

One only needs to look at our children in the school system today to see the depth of our predicament. Their challenges are earthshaking compared to what I faced at the same age. You don't have to look very far to find disturbing statistics. It's unsettling to witness grammar school students grappling with the fear of mass shootings within their classrooms. [1] Middle schoolers are navigating complex gender identity questions, a challenge unheard of in previous generations. [2] Even college students are tragically resorting to suicide at alarming rates. [3] We have a high school in our backyard with a suicide rate four times higher than the national average.

I often see parents and teachers from this high school while working at Trader Joe's, and everything I see tells me they are doing a great job with these kids. But the burden remains. The anxiety associated with living in today's world is literally killing us.

We need a way to cope. *Slowing down* is a part of it and can surely help the long-term view. But as my kids would quickly rebut, I need to get through today first.

Sitting

Learning to pay attention to the moment is a valuable tool for dealing with our burdensome world. "Being present" is a nonjudgmental phrase that allows you to experience the here and now. Another common term is mindfulness, which Wikipedia defines as "The awareness that can emerge from paying attention to the present moment" [4]. Essentially, it's about gaining a sense of dominion over your experience of the current moment.

We miss so much about ourselves daily because of our desire for forward motion. As humans, we constantly strive to improve and get ahead in life. But amid our progress, we tend to miss what we feel in our innermost being.

"Sitting" is a simple form of being present I often recommend to my coaching clients as a practice for learning to pause amid their hectic and chaotic lives. [5] I discovered the sitting practice in my training to become a New Ventures West "Integral Coach." Our instructor requested that we spend 30 minutes *every* day sitting for the *entire year* of our training. Thirty minutes a day seemed far-fetched to me. I quickly did the math to tell the instructor he was crazy if he thought I had a surplus of 182 hours this year just to sit!

Fast-forward one year and sitting became a personal highlight of the training class for me. I worked up to 30 minutes a day in quiet solitude, ultimately finding this time was transformative in developing myself as a human being who could help others find themselves. Sitting allowed me the freedom to connect with my spiritual center while feeding my soul in the stillness. I cannot recommend it enough (even if only *five* minutes a day).

"How wonderful it is to have a moment in time where we don't have to be anyone." — Anonymous

Today, sitting in the early morning for 15 to 20 minutes is a daily ritual. I make a cup of green tea and then retreat into my "sanctuary" in the dark quiet of dawn. This time spent alone in perfect peace calms my heart for whatever God has in store for me that day. I have always felt prayer should be a two-way conversation with God. Sitting provides me the margin to *listen* to what God might have to say. I come out of these sessions feeling refreshed and encouraged, with a sense of purpose for the upcoming day. The days when I miss my sitting practice (which are rare) are often the days I feel the most out of tune with the world around me.

Sitting in the Surf

The ability to sit is also a critical skill for surfing. It isn't easy to properly position the surfboard for an incoming wave if you cannot effectively sit upright while doing the "eggbeater" motion with your legs to maintain balance. It often makes me laugh when we introduce a "first-timer" to surfing, only to witness their struggle to maintain a seated position on the board in the water. Suppressing my urge to giggle out loud, I watch as they repeatedly tip over in their quest for equilibrium. Learning to sit on a surfboard proves to be a humbling experience indeed.

I will admit I am not naturally inclined to just sit on my board in the water, waiting for a wave. I get a bit anxious during a long lull between sets. If there is a wave anywhere in sight, I am likely to paddle after it. Isn't that the point of surfing – to catch waves? Yet, as I have matured over the years, I am learning to appreciate the time seated on my board. It can be a rewarding, meditative experience. In my stillness, I sense the presence of God amid His astonishing creation surrounding me. The ocean can be a magnificent sanctuary for being present.

Recently, my son Matthew and I went to Pleasure Point (Santa Cruz) at sunset, and I experienced this in an unforgettable way. I was able to paddle into a space where no other surfers were around me. As I scanned the horizon for waves, I could appreciate the surrounding elegance of nature as the sun began fading below a thin line of clouds on the horizon. The streaked cirrus clouds above me lit up with bright orange and fluorescent yellow behind a darkening purple sky. An endless bathtub of navy-blue salt water carried me into another world as I heard sea otters cracking open their fresh seafood dinner in the distance. The lull of the waves elevated my sense of peace and tranquility as if I was floating above it all. A seal quietly popped its head above water, as if on cue, to greet me just a few feet away. I settled into my sitting pose to soak in the unfolding experience as if watching a movie. I did not have to be anyone. I only had to be. God was speaking, and I was fully present to hear Him.

It all soaked deep into my soul, and I prayed the lull would last. I had stopped to smell the roses; it was truly a slice of Heaven from God.

Be still and know that I am God.
— Psalm 46:10 (NIV)

Notes

1. According to the Pew Research Center, 2018, many U.S. teens fear a shooting could happen at their school, and most parents share their concerns.

   https://www.pewresearch.org/fact-tank/2018/04/18/a-majority-of-u-s-teens-fear-a-shooting-could-happen-at-their-school-and-most-parents-share-their-concern/

2. Gender Dysphoria in Young People: A Model of Chronic Stress, 2021.

   https://www.karger.com/Article/FullText/520361

3. According to the American College Health Association (ACHA), 2021, suicide is currently the second most common cause of death among college students in the U.S.

   https://www.verywellmind.com/suicide-rates-overstated-in-people-with-depression-2330503

   Rosiek A, Rosiek-Kryszewska A, Leksowski Ł, Leksowski K., 2016, Chronic stress and suicidal thinking among medical students.

4. Wikipedia: https://en.wikipedia.org/wiki/Mindfulness

5. Link for instructions on sitting:
   www.SurfingForBalance.com/resources

24. Marathon Faith

Be faithful and leave the results to God.
— Amish Proverb

In between surf sessions, I love to run.

Surfing served as my escape valve from the relentless stress of Silicon Valley, but running was my boat anchor, helping me to keep my priorities intact amidst all the madness around me. I could only get to Santa Cruz to surf once a week at best while my running shoes were in the trunk of my car every day. All I needed was a free hour, and I could sneak in a quick 5K on the levees behind our office and be back in the saddle as a new man, refreshed from head to toe. When I look back at the peaks and valleys of my Silicon Valley tech career, running was often my saving grace.

The boundless physical joy and mental solace of running throughout the years are beyond measure. Whether embarking on a morning sojourn amidst the serenity of Rancho San Antonio Park in the foothills of the Santa Cruz Mountains or hitting the Baylands Nature Preserve trails during lunch, running served as my sanctuary from the relentless pace of riding the Silicon Valley Express. Lacing up for a run liberates me from immediate worries, channeling my focus inward to push my physical boundaries. I emerge from each run feeling thoroughly revitalized due to immersion in fresh air, warm sun, and the splendor of nature.

During certain runs, a deep sense of inner consciousness unexpectedly descends upon me like an unpredictable mist. Despite the physical exertion of running, I slowly enter this state of being, allowing me access into the recesses of my soul. My consciousness becomes detached from the act of running as I lose awareness of my surroundings and the physical effort exerted. This experience is beautiful, akin to what some describe as the runner's high, yet for me, it transcends the mere physicality of the run. It brings me great peace as if I am in communion with God while floating through His magnificent creation. Emerging from this state, I feel a profound sense of self-assurance and confidence in God's plan for my life. While glancing at my watch may reveal the stats on my run, I recognize something far more profound has occurred – it has nourished my soul.

I caught the running bug in the 1970s, during the height of the running boom in the U.S., spurred by Frank Shorter's gold medal win in the Olympic Marathon, the first for an American in 64 years. My first organized race was a 10K at the Dana Point Turkey Trot on Thanksgiving Day in 1979. Anyone who knows me is aware of my *passion* for Turkey Trots.[1] Well, it all started there.

I will *never* forget that race in 1979. My roommate Brad Sarvak and I sprinted off the starting line at the very front and had the race leaders in view for the first two miles. We had *no idea* what we were doing. My former high school track coach, John Blair [2], led the lead pack on his mini motorcycle as we heard the mile splits being called out at a pace that made it clear we were in deep trouble. And then, between miles two and three, it hit.

The last three miles are cemented in my memory as the most excruciating miles of my running career. No matter how much I backed off, the pain only intensified. It felt like it would hurt even if I walked. I didn't throw up, but I sure wanted to. Reaching the finish line at mile 6.2 was pure agony. I remember Coach Blair asking me afterward why I hadn't run on the team in high school. I don't recall exactly what I said, but it must have been something like, "Because it hurts too much." My friend Brad Sarvak was there to back me up on that. I felt the aftermath of the race in my gut for a week.

I never had that problem with surfing.

The Dana Point Turkey Trot soon became an annual tradition. As much as I labored in the effort each year, something kept pulling me back to run it again. Part of it was testing my endurance to find out how hard I could push the pace. It *always* hurt, but I felt high as a kite after the race for enduring the suffering of those 6.2 miles. Another draw was the post-race party, which got pretty lively in the pre-celebration atmosphere of Thanksgiving – the draft beer helped. Eating my fill of turkey and pumpkin pie later in the day was like the whipped cream on the pumpkin pie that made it all worth the effort.

I soon found myself running 10k races almost every weekend with my good friend, Ed Mantini. Ed was an Alberto Salazar look-alike who seemed to run almost as fast. He challenged me each week to lower my 10K time while introducing me to DMSO [3] as our go-to cure for virtually any running injury we came across. DMSO was essential to keeping our weekly mileage consistently high. We pushed each other every weekend at local 5k and 10k races to see who could come out on top. This friendly rivalry stretched us both to reach new heights in our running.

The Marathon

I soon signed up for my first marathon, the "Leatherneck Marathon," at the El Toro Marine Base in Orange County. I distinctly remember hitting the 20-mile mark and thinking, *Oh, this is what they meant by "the wall".* . . Those last three miles of the first Dana Point Turkey Trot came right back to me – *times two*. Nothing in running can compare to those last six miles of your first marathon. Pure agony and guts alone got me to the finish line.

Before long, I was addicted to the carbo-loading diet and the high-mileage training the marathon required. It was time to try and qualify for the renowned Boston Marathon, which required a *fast* marathon (sub-2:50) to get in. [4] Anyone who has run Boston would surely agree the excitement, energy, and goodwill surrounding the event are unmatched in marathon circles. Bill Rodgers, who won Boston four times (1975, 1978-1980), said it well:

"...The marathon is the king of sports. And certainly, Boston is the king of marathons."

Rodgers wrote the book on "marathoning" back then [5] while also winning the New York City Marathon four times in a row (1976-1979). His success propelled me, and his book became my training bible. I soon learned how to navigate the 26.2-mile beast and began chiseling down my finishing times to attain my goal. Thank you, Bill!

The Pace

I see distinct parallels between the marathon and my life here on Earth. I can sense the challenges ahead as I cross the twenty-mile mark in my life for that final push to the finish line. My pace *is* slowing, yet my focus on *finishing strong* is still there. These are the most important miles of my life. In marathoning jargon, my race has just begun.

A successful marathon requires careful planning to achieve a steady pace that matches an intended (and realistic) finishing time. If I went out too fast those first 20 miles, eventually, I would crash and burn. The goal is to keep within that pacing range for 26.2 miles. By the time you reach mile 20, it becomes a grueling effort of concentration and physical stamina to stay at the intended pace.

At the 1994 California International Marathon in Sacramento, I learned this pacing principle the hard way. The weather was near perfect, and the first 20 miles blazed by, nearly 30 seconds per mile faster than my targeted pace. I was flying high and decided I was having one of those dream days.

Ha.

I stopped for a cup of water at mile 20 before the bridge leading to the finish line at the state capitol, and that was it. I was *done* running. I was forced to *walk* all the way to mile 25 when a good friend, Paul Fick, kicked my butt (literally) to make sure I shuffled it in with him for the home stretch. I could not lift my feet above the ground. That wall seemed insurmountable. At one point, a guy called out to me from his porch as I hobbled by:

"Dude, you'll need a new pair of shoes before you finish if you keep that up!"

I did not think that was funny at the time (now I do.). I was a physical wreck for several days after that race. The experience completely humbled me. I learned a hard lesson that day: the marathon requires a certain amount of caution and strategic planning to achieve your goal beyond the physical training. To go out and run with your gut can lead to disaster.

This pacing principle carries over into life. Our life is not a sprint. Yet, most of us today will admit to going too fast much of the time, especially during those early years. Even our kids realize this. Technology is stealing our margins and enabling us to do more than our bodies (and brains) were designed for. Like the marathon, if we don't slow down, eventually, we will crash. I've seen it many times throughout my tech career. Like a bonk in the marathon, it is not a pretty sight.

As a life coach, I aim to improve my clients' capacity and set a pace they can maintain for the long-term view of life. It is mostly about easing up on commitments to allow the body time to rest and recover. I found out myself how difficult that can be. Getting "downsized" was not exactly how I would have planned it, but I now look back and view that time as a gift from God. My pace may be slower now, but I have confidence in the race plan to finish strong.

The Finish Line

The goal of the marathon is to finish, which requires a singular focus on the finish line. Nothing else matters. All the rewards of your training are waiting for you at mile 26.2. The euphoria of crossing the finish line is worth all the blood, sweat, and tears you put into getting there. I liken it to running as if you are a racehorse with blinders on. To look at or think about anything beyond the finish is simply a distraction that can cause you to lose concentration and potentially crash. Crossing the finish line turns the whole event into a joyful celebration. As my wife and most other women would attest with childbirth, in the end, the prize cancels out the extreme suffering you endured to get there. The victory parade begins, no matter how much you hurt.

I had never felt more joy and satisfaction at the end of a marathon than when my son Matthew and I embraced at the end of the 2016 St. George Marathon (his first). The tears were flowing. It was a wondrous moment as we bear-hugged each other, drenched in the sweat and pain of our efforts. We savored the victory together. Marathons don't get any better than that.

War Heroes at the 2016 St. George Marathon (Mike, Matthew, Lou, Bill – "Finished!")

The Bible tells us our finish line in Heaven will be even better. What awaits us at the finish line of life will be beyond anything we can experience here on Earth. My heart's desire is to cross that finish line strong in this life and hear the words, "Well done good and faithful servant!" [6]

The euphoria of crossing the finish line into Heaven is something I can only wonder about. It will exceed what our minds can imagine. [7] God has mapped out an eternal destination that defies logic as we understand it. Heaven has turned the tide in my life here on Earth towards eternity. My focus now is solely on the finish line banner. I want to spend every day I have left in preparation for the day when I can cross that line into Heaven.

You may be asking how I can be so sure of this. How can we know we will go to Heaven when we die? For me, it boils down to faith. *Marathon* Faith. Jesus paid the price for our salvation. By simply accepting the gift of His death on the cross, Heaven is a sure thing. It *is* that easy. [8]

The Bible is very clear about Heaven. There are hundreds of references to what it will be like. The Book of Revelation paints a particularly stunning description at the end of the Bible when Heaven and Earth come together as one. [9] Heaven is as clear a finish line at the end of life as the 26.2-mile banner is to the marathoner. I have my horse blinders on and refuse to consider any other option. Heaven is the finish line that matters. I am planning to come in running strong. It's getting closer every day. Don't miss it!

As C.S. Lewis once said:

> "Aim at Heaven and you will get Earth thrown in. Aim at Earth and you get neither. "

See the Appendix V for Mike's "Going to Heaven" booklist to expand your horizons on what might be possible in Heaven.

Do you not know that in a race all the runners run, but only one gets the prize? Run in such a way as to get the prize!
— 1 Corinthians 9:24 (NIV)

Notes

1. Mike Mulkey is the founder of the Mountain View High School "Spartan Turkey Trot," which will celebrate its 15th year in 2024 (SpartanTurkeyTrot.com).

2. Coach John Blair, a Los Angeles Times Millennium Hall of Fame inductee, was a true innovator in the Corona del Mar High School (CdMHS) running community. Aside from coaching cross country and track at CdMHS for 18 years (1965-1982), Coach Blair pioneered ideas for road running events before 10K and 5K road races came into being.

3. Dimethyl Sulfoxide (DMSO) has been a trusted topical remedy in my family for decades. It all began when my grandmother, Oa, shared how it eased her arthritis in the 1970s. Following suit, Dad found relief for his tennis elbow in the early 1980s. DMSO was a sure cure for nagging running injuries for Ed and me back in the 1980s, and I still use it to this day.

4. After the 1979 Boston Marathon, officials lowered the qualifying time for men under 40 from 3:00 to 2:50.

   Derderian, Tom. Boston Marathon: *The History of the World's Premier Running Event*. Champaign, IL: Human Kinetics, 1996. (Preface)

5. Rodgers, Bill. *Marathoning*. New York: Random House, 1982. Bill Rodgers won the Boston Marathon four times (1975, 1978-1980) and the New York City Marathon four times (1976-1979).

6. Matthew 25:23 (NIV)

   "His master replied, 'Well done, good and faithful servant! You have been faithful with a few things; I will put you in charge of many things. Come and share your master's happiness!'"

7. 1 Corinthians 2:9 (NIV)

    "However, as it is written: 'What no eye has seen, what no ear has heard, and what no human mind has conceived' – the things God has prepared for those who love Him."

8. See Appendix IV for a prayer to receive Jesus Christ as your savior.

9. Revelation 21:1-4 (NIV)

    "Then I saw a new Heaven and a new Earth, for the first Heaven and the first Earth had passed away, and there was no longer any sea. I saw the Holy City, the new Jerusalem, coming down out of Heaven from God, prepared as a bride beautifully dressed for her husband. And I heard a loud voice from the throne saying, 'Look! God's dwelling place is now among the people, and he will dwell with them. They will be his people, and God Himself will be with them and be their God. He will wipe every tear from their eyes. There will be no more death or mourning or crying or pain, for the old order of things has passed away.'"

7th Wave – Kicking Out

- Knowing my future is secure in Heaven as I prepare to kick out.

25. The Future is Secure

If you're going through hell, keep your eyes on Heaven.
— René Schlaepfer (pastor, author, speaker)

Let's cut to the chase. I wrote this book to confirm your future is secure. Despite all the craziness in our world today, God and His Word remain utterly trustworthy. Nothing else can match the Bible (including Google *and* AI) for speaking the truth. The Bible is unequivocal about our future. Death is *not* the end of our story. Heaven will be better than anything we can imagine here on Earth. The Bible is crystal clear about that. I am not sure there has ever been a more critical time to be reading the best-selling book of all time (i.e., the Bible).

One major issue we must confront is the presence of evil in our world today. Sin and Satan are real and present threats to Heaven's citizens while they live on earth. The Bible states "the whole world is under the control of the evil one." [1] Satan has been present from the very beginning with Adam and Eve. [2] The Apostle Peter described Satan as "a hungry, roaring lion, looking for some victim to deceive and tear apart." [3] Just turn on the evening news, and you will see fresh evidence of this every day. I can't even answer my phone or respond to an email without concern that someone may be trying to deceive me. We are increasingly under attack from all directions. This is a profound spiritual battle, much larger than the physical battles we see raging on the nightly news.

Modern Society has lost respect for the Bible. It has been banned from our schools and is no longer playing a leading role in guiding humanity's choices. The fact that prayer has been outlawed from our public schools since 1962 is not helping. [4] The results are telling. Christianity has been driven to the margins of society. For example, I am reading a book (nonfiction) in which the author describes the Bible as "archaic, old, and meaningless in modern society." That thinking is all too common today. The need for Christians to be serious about their faith has never been greater. Without God and His deep wisdom and guidance as our anchor, we interpret life with only human insight, leaving us hanging by a thread.

My goal with this book has been to change that trajectory by injecting the promise of Heaven into the world. Heaven derails Satan's goal of destroying our future. The whole reason God sent Jesus to Earth was to conquer death and to assure us about Heaven, which includes victory over death. [5] The Bible assures us that Jesus defeats Satan in the end (Revelation 20:10). By fixing our gaze on the eternal home God is preparing for us, we spoil Satan's plan for our demise. The evil one does not want us to believe there *is* a Heaven. He does not want us to read the truth of scripture. Heaven gives us the hope the evil one wants to destroy. Heaven gives us security about where we are going. Heaven will be a world without Satan; God assures us it will be better than we can imagine.

I recently had a discussion with a customer at Trader Joe's that demonstrated how far we have strayed from God's word in our thinking. One of the things I enjoy about being in the store is that I gain a pulse on our community. Here is the story as it happened.

"We are going to let them decide . . ."

A young lady came to my line at the cash register with a shopping cart of groceries. She was pregnant and clearly ready to have the baby any day (or hour). I struck up a conversation about how she was doing as I scanned her groceries. I enjoy talking to expectant parents to relive the wonderful memories of our two children being born. I asked her the usual questions: When are you due? What hospital? First child? How are you feeling? It all went smoothly until I asked,

"Do you know if it is a boy or girl?"

She paused as I continued to scan the groceries. Then she looked up at me and responded, "Well, we are going to let *them* decide."

I continued bagging her groceries while trying to figure out what she meant. Then it hit me: She would not identify the sex of their baby by whether it came out as a boy or a girl. She would let *them* decide their sex.

Oh my. How sad.

I quickly finished bagging the groceries and sent her on her way with good wishes for the delivery. But it was hard for me to reconcile what had just happened. I have thought about it many times since.

I stand behind the Bible as my only source of truth. Our life is a sacred gift from God, and the Bible answers how we should use it. God's Word looks beyond today's trouble to embrace eternity's victory.

Satan is trying to drag us into the abyss. His goal is to see us lose hope, proclaiming the Bible is outdated and irrelevant. Heaven is the last thing he wants us to think about. Heaven destroys his plan for us. It's his worst nightmare.

I do believe something unrivaled awaits me in Heaven. The very best we may have experienced here on Earth cannot measure up to what God has planned. [6] Experiencing a sunset at the beach, a wildflower in the mountains, or a pelican riding the draft of a breaking wave are just appetizers for what God has in store for us in Heaven. It will be a place of complete sensory delight and breathtaking splendor with personal joy in relationships beyond our grasp.

The evil one won't take away my hope. My future is secure in Jesus Christ.

Let me know how I can pray for you. [7]

For the wisdom of this world is foolishness in God's sight.
    — 1 Corinthians 3:19 (NIV)

Notes

1. 1 John 5:19 (NIV)

   "We know that we are children of God, and that the whole world is under the control of the evil one."

2. Genesis 3:1 (NIV)

   "Now the serpent was more crafty than any of the wild animals the Lord God had made. He said to the woman, 'Did God really say, "You must not eat from any tree in the garden?"'"

3. 1Peter 5:8 (TLB)

   "Be careful – watch out for attacks from Satan, your great enemy. He prowls around like a hungry, roaring lion, looking for some victim to tear apart."

4. Prayer was effectively outlawed from public schools in the United States, with the Supreme Court ruling in the case of *Engel v. Vitale* in 1962.

5. 1 John 3:8 (NIV)

   "The one who does what is sinful is of the devil, because the devil has been sinning from the beginning. The reason the Son of God appeared was to destroy the devil's work."

6. Revelation 21:4 (NIV)

   "He will wipe every tear from their eyes. There will be no more death or mourning or crying or pain, for the old order of things has passed away."

7. Click "Contact Mike" at SurfingForBalance.com.

26. Kicking Out

He is no fool who gives what he cannot keep to gain what he cannot lose.
— Jim Elliot (Christian Missionary)

American evangelist Billy Graham (1918-2018) was asked what the biggest surprise in his life had been. He quickly replied, "The brevity of life. Almost before we know it, the years have passed, and life is almost over." [1]

My life has *flown* by. It seems like just yesterday I was out surfing San Onofre with Dad on my Corky Carroll "Super Mini" surfboard. Before I know it, God will soon be calling. In the meantime, I try to trust God to help me navigate the peaks and valleys on the road ahead. Finishing strong in God's eyes is my goal. I am preparing for a life with Him for eternity in Heaven.

A surfer who rides a wave to its proper completion with a successful kick out has a similar anticipation of finishing strong. The kick out enables you to surf your way out of the wave with a true sense of completion to the ride, leaving you in control of your destiny for your next ride. The kick out transitions you from the wave you were riding to paddling back out for another. It is *not* a simple maneuver in surfing, especially if you are riding a longboard. [2]

Before the advent of the surf leash (and subsequent shortboard revolution) in the late 1960s, knowing how to kick out was a fundamental requirement for serious surfing. You could judge a surfer's ability solely by the effectiveness of their kick outs. The better the kick out, the better a surfer they are (almost without exception). The more skilled surfers had figured out a good kick out got you more waves as you were quickly back out into the lineup.

Kicking out is nearly a lost art in surfing today. I rarely see a surfer cleanly exit the wave they are riding to go over the lip with momentum in the right direction for a quick paddle back out (while checking for any waves coming).

With surf leashes ruling the lineups today, it is more common to see a surfer end a ride by simply diving or jumping off their board into the white water without concern for losing their surfboard. It works, but it would be more likely to score points in a diving competition than in a surfing contest. The term "kook cord" (for the surf leash) can be attributed partly to those types of kick outs. The style and finesse of surfing are completely lost.

Competing in the San Onofre Surfing Contest in the 1960s taught me the proper technique of the kick out. The judges rewarded surfers who could execute a clean and controlled kick out. Kicking out at the right place and time of a ride demonstrated good judgment while controlling your board to exit the wave cleanly. Extra points could be attained for a high degree of difficulty when exiting with your board from a wave closing out or breaking in a critical section. Kicking out was your final act to demonstrate your surfing abilities to the judges. A missed kick out could involve a time-consuming swim back to the beach and paddle back out. At San Onofre, that would usually spell disaster for your chances to advance to the next round.

Kicking Out in Life

Finishing strong in the life we have been given here on Earth means seeking God to the very end. [3] That is God's idea of a successful kick out. He wants to see a life well lived, denying self and trusting in Him. When we reach the end of this ride on earth, the love of Christ will surpass all knowledge. We are truly unable to form a mental image of how good it will be. So, we carry on in this life, longing to hear the words, "Well done, good and faithful servant" at Heaven's gate. [4]

I was working at Trader Joe's on May 9, 2020, when a fellow crew member told me a 26-year-old surfer had been fatally attacked by a shark while surfing at Sand Dollar Beach, just south of Manresa State Beach (near Santa Cruz). My son Matthew and I surf at Sand Dollar, and I knew he had been there the day before. I immediately called Matt's cell phone. It went to voicemail. I then called his work. After what felt like an eternity on hold, he picked up the phone and greeted me.

So grateful.

The victim was a local Santa Cruz surfer and shaper, Ben Kelly. Thinking it was my son, even if just for a minute, gave me insight into the unimaginable pain Ben's family and friends were going through.

I soon learned more about Ben and was deeply touched by his story. Ben was a seasoned surfer and board shaper who started his own surfboard company in Santa Cruz (Ben Kelly Surfboards). He graduated Summa Cum Laude from Vanguard University in Southern California, where he was awarded the McNaughton Award, its highest honor for business and management students. He had recently celebrated his third wedding anniversary with his wife, Katie, whom he met at Vanguard.

Ben was stoked about the life God had given him. He was active in the Capitola Village Business Improvement Association, Twin Lakes Church in Aptos, and Calvary Chapel in Capitola. At one point, he was selling surfboards to support the missionary work he was involved with in Africa.

The Santa Cruz County Board of Supervisors declared that May 21 (Ben's birthday) would be "Ben Kelly Day." The proclamation stated:

"Ben practiced his belief that surfing was so much more than just catching waves – it was about the people he met and the continuous grand adventures that made it fun while blessing others along the way."

I had never met Ben and only came upon his story through surfing. Yet, he rose for me as the modern-day equivalent of "the greatest generation." Ben's love of Jesus was front and center in his life. He had that surfer's "stoke" about him, which some called his good vibes, but those close to him knew his faith fed it.

Ben did not just talk about his faith; he exemplified it through his character. In the words of a close friend, "Ben lived the way Christ wanted us to live." His opening line on his LinkedIn account boldly demonstrated this ("About"):

"Hello, my name is Ben Kelly. Some of my life passions include: a love for my Savior Jesus Christ . . ."

Ben was not hiding who he believed would save him on his day of reckoning. [5] He finished strong. In the book of Matthew, Jesus spoke about the importance of doing God's will to reveal His love and presence in the world:

"Not everyone who says to Me, 'Lord, Lord,' will enter the kingdom of Heaven, but he who does the will of My Father who is in Heaven will enter" (Matthew 7:21, NIV).

Jesus called us to embrace the words of Scripture, so they are central to our daily lives. He said true wisdom is all about actions of love, mercy, and peace [6]. It is not enough to say, "Lord, Lord."

Ben Kelly has both inspired and challenged me in this respect. Though he never saw it coming, Ben kicked out of this life with full control over his destiny. He had hope in a God who created the Heavens and the Earth. He wanted to live his life honoring that God, knowing his rewards would be in Heaven. His future was secure, and his kick out was perfect. I believe God gave him a ten.

Ben has motivated me to finish strong. I look forward to the day I can paddle out with him.

"Well done, good and faithful servant!"
(Photo by Baker Carroll)

What is your life? You are a mist that appears for a little while and then vanishes.
— James 4:14 (NIV)

Notes

1. Graham, Billy. *Just as I Am: The Autobiography of Billy Graham*. San Francisco: HarperOne, 2011.

2. Longboards are generally considered to be surfboards over nine feet long. The difference in navigating a successful kick out is dramatic. For example, Dad rode a 10'9" Bob Simmons Plywood Foam surfboard (called a "Foam Sandwich") at Malibu in the late 1940s (see surfingforbalance.com). To effectively kick out on that board, Dad learned to drag a foot over the side of the board to act as a rudder (as you would with a paddle on a kayak). The board wouldn't just turn out of the wave on its own.

3. Philippians 3:14 (TLB)

    "I strain to reach the end of the race and receive the prize for which God is calling us up to Heaven because of what Christ Jesus did for us."

4. Matthew 25:23 (NIV)

    "His master replied, 'Well done, good and faithful servant! You have been faithful with a few things; I will put you in charge of many things. Come and share your master's happiness!'"

5. One tribute read at Ben's memorial service stated:

    The most memorable thing about Ben was his unashamed, unrelenting passion for his faith and his relationship with Jesus. I don't say this to somehow selfishly reassure myself or others that he's passed on to Heaven. I don't have to wonder whether he knew Jesus, or whether his faith was secure. It was. Everybody knew it. He truly lived his faith out. In nearly every conversation I ever had with him, he tied God and the redeeming love of Jesus into it.

6. James 3:17-18 (NIV)

    "But the wisdom that comes from Heaven is first of all pure; then peace-loving, considerate, submissive, full of mercy and good fruit, impartial and sincere. Peacemakers who sow in peace reap a harvest of righteousness."

8th Wave – The Perfect Wave

- My imperfect sketch of surfing in Heaven.

27. Surfing in Heaven

Heaven walks among us.
— Ralph Waldo Emerson (American writer, philosopher, and poet)

Surfing in Heaven. Outrageous thought.

Or is it?

In the late 1940s, when Dad surfed Malibu with his small band of World War II vets who were fortunate to have returned home, he told me he never went surfing in the winter. They did not have wetsuits then, so it was too cold to paddle out. Anyone who knew Dad would vouch for his hostility toward cold water (or cold weather, for that matter). After fleeing the winters of Newport Beach and moving to Kailua-Kona, Hawaii, in the 1980s, he would tell us even the winters in Kona were getting uncomfortably cool for him. What? Yet I knew it was a serious matter when he asked for house slippers and sweatshirts for Christmas.

Dad recounted how this elite crowd of surfing pioneers would stand at the shoreline of Malibu on a crisp winter day, mesmerized by the sight of flawless waves cascading onto the shore untouched by any surfer. That poignant image has since been etched into my memory, igniting vivid fantasies of what it would have been like to venture into those pristine waves clad in the warmth of my trusty O'Neill wetsuit. The mere thought of paddling out into the solitude of Malibu's waters during that era totally gets me stoked.

It would have been a surfer's *paradise.*

For me, Heaven brings the surfing paradise into sight. I can vividly imagine waves so flawlessly formed, reminiscent of Malibu's finest, rolling in harmoniously, untouched by any other soul. I am giddy with anticipation to consider what might be awaiting us there. Getting a clearer picture of my future in Heaven has completely changed my perspective on life. For a God who moves mountains, [1] perfect waves in the world hereafter seem well within reach.

In Jesus' final hours with His disciples before His death, He told them He was preparing a mansion for each of them in Heaven [2] and that they would have great rewards waiting for them when they arrived.

I believe my mansion in Heaven will be near a beach, and my rewards will include surfing. That seems like an easy one for a God who created it *all* in the first place. [3] To look at it from a surfer's perspective, if Kelly Slater (eleven-time world champion surfer) can create a near-perfect 6-foot barreling wave in a desert in California's Central Valley (kswaveco.com), could not our great God fulfill the promise of Heaven with something even better? I am betting on it and looking forward to getting wet as soon as I get there. Grab your wax; I am excited and anticipate you will be with me for the ride.

My portrayal undoubtedly will fall far short of the experience Heaven will offer. Nothing in our human experience can reach the divine joy, beauty, and love awaiting us there. I pray this gives you hope and the will to accept God's gift to ensure you will be there to paddle out with me.

Jesus' final words to the thief who was hanging on the cross next to Him provide the perfect opening to my imperfect sketch of what this experience of surfing in Heaven could be:

"Truly I tell you, today you will be with me in paradise" (Luke 23:43, NIV).

My fascination with this idea of surfing in Heaven has been running wild in my mind for years. As God placed it on my heart to envision what awaits me in the life hereafter, a sketch came together of how my odyssey would go. You can think of it as a dream, but for me, it flowed quite naturally and felt right. In the words of Rebecca Ruter Springer, [4]

"I submit this imperfect sketch of a most perfect vision."

My Imperfect Sketch

My time has come. God is calling me home. I've waited a lifetime for this moment.

As angels arrive, my spirit gently separates from my physical body. Drifting effortlessly above my earthly home, I ascend into a tunnel of bright light. Accelerating through the cosmos, vivid memories flood my consciousness – moments with loved ones, the joys and sorrows that shaped my existence on Earth. Forgotten fragments of childhood emerge with vivid clarity, each memory a vibrant illustration imbued with the sensory richness of sound, scent, and taste. Tranquility washes over me as I see every moment fitting perfectly into place, filling me with profound peace and joy. It is well with my soul. I am grateful for God's hand in every part of it.

My sense of time disappears as my faithful Grandma Oa appears before me. Oh *my*. She is so young and beautiful, her smile wide and her face bright. I delight to see her younger than I knew her.

"I am so happy to welcome you, Mike," she says. "Everyone is very excited to see you."

I know why without asking. Grandma faithfully prayed for me for so many years. Tears of joy come to my eyes as I hug her. It goes beyond words to let her know how miraculous it is to see her again. We tightly embrace, feeling the love of God between us. Words are exchanged without talking. It's as if we know each other's thoughts before we think them. Our communication is perfect. There is no misunderstanding. *Everything* is right.

She leads me down a long path of the most beautiful grass I have ever seen – a brilliant shade of green that rivals the fairways at Pebble Beach. It feels like velvet under my feet as we walk together. A wondrous variety of plants and flowers surround us, so bright and colorful I want to stop and inspect each one. They are perfect and appear freshly bloomed. Everything is pure and clean as if bathed in an afternoon shower. Tall, majestic trees tower above us with hanging branches like weeping willows laden with flowers of every variety and color imaginable. Beyond the trees, I see orchards of ripe fruit-bearing trees with a translucent river meandering through. Waterfalls roar in the distance from lush mountains capped with pure white snow. Small birds in the trees are singing joyous songs of Heaven's praise. They drench me with their melodies from above like a mountain waterfall. It is breathtaking. The music embraces my soul as I behold an overwhelming feeling of harmony with nature. [5] The fragrance of the forest around us refreshes my sense of pine needles and evergreen trees. I have never felt more alive in my life.

I want to stop and explore the depth of what I am experiencing, but we continue walking, almost floating, among this stunning scenery. The flawless beauty astounds me; it's as if a Master Gardener tends to every detail. Our path leads us to a babbling creek, its waters crystal clear, cascading over a bed adorned with glistening stones of gold, silver, jasper, emerald, and pearl – a treasure trove worthy of a pirate's bounty. Soft melodies embrace my soul as we wade along the creek, immersed in the moment's splendor. Time loses its grip; I could walk here forever.

The sky above explodes with brilliant color, eclipsing even the brightest noonday sun, though its source remains unseen. A golden radiance saturates the atmosphere like the afterglow of a brilliant sunset, yet infinitely more radiant. Grandma and I are not talking, yet our communication is complete. She knows what I am feeling. "It is well, Mike," she assures me. Indeed, all is well.

Our path opens onto a vast expanse of beach with sand like freshly fallen snow. I pause to contemplate how it could be. The sand is warm and sneaks between my toes to comfort me. The air is soft and balmy, giving me energy and vitality. A light breeze feathers my face. I want to lie down and soak all this in, reminiscent of carefree days at Big Corona State Beach from my youth.

As we cross the pristine sand with freshly laid footprints, my gaze falls upon a structure reminiscent of the beloved surf shack at the San Onofre Surfing Club. Its design is impeccable, adorned with wooden surfboards, and crowned by a simple yet striking white cross atop a modest steeple. I feel drawn to it as we walk side by side.

Approaching the structure, I see it is made from living trees resembling palm trees firmly rooted in the sandy foundation. Their leaves form a natural canopy, filtering the right amount of light into the interior. Dazzling multicolored flowers, like Hawaiian leis, adorn the branches, intricately weaving around the steeple and roof. The air is saturated with fragrances reminiscent of gardenias, enveloping me as I step inside.

Euphoria overwhelms me as a hoard of family and friends are there to welcome me home. It is a reunion like no other. One by one, they greet and embrace me in mutual joy and wonder of shared experiences. Words cannot capture the depth of my emotions. I see Mom; how glorious she looks. Her smile and laugh knock me over. We embrace as never before. Then Grandpa Cannon, Aunt Kathryn, Grandma Mary and Grandpa John wrap me in their arms. It's as if they all have been friends forever. When I see Aunt Sally and Aunt Norma, my delight is breathtaking. Friends from our church, our former pastor Doug Goins, and even classmates from high school are there. It's a surreal connection and reunion to them beyond earthly words.

Then I see the coach himself, John Wooden. Oh *my*. He looks at me with that Coach Wooden sparkle in his eye and says, once again,

"The most important thing in the world is family and love."

Everyone is jubilant. The feeling of love consumes me. We gather in the delight of it all for longer than I know as more loved ones continue to trickle in. Amidst the party, our cherished dogs, Riley and Redwood, playfully push their way through the many people to nuzzle me with cold, wet noses, tails wagging with zeal for affection. I immediately roll onto the ground to grab them in playful hugs. Nothing could be better. I hear the words singing in my soul,

"His love endures forever." [6]

Here, time stands still. Nobody is rushed or in a hurry to leave. I have lived my whole life for this. I don't have to pinch myself. I really am in Heaven, and I don't want to leave.

Surfing in Heaven

Beyond our gathering, I notice what appears to be an ocean of water with perfect eight-foot tubes curling in. Whoa!

I move in that direction, savoring the warmth of the sand under my feet. Nearing the water's edge, I see three surfboards lying in the sand. I am overwhelmed by the scene before me. Angels are singing my praises to God as I approach the three boards.

I see Dad next to his Bob Simmons Foam Sandwich surfboard. We embrace. Joyful tears run down my cheeks. He is healthy and robust with a tan as dark as a native Hawaiian. I am so glad to see him. Without speaking, he tells me he is sorry. Words cannot express my wonder and joy. There are no longer any barriers between us. It all makes sense now.

Next to Dad is Uncle Charles, his face painted like a Māori warrior, looking as if he is right off the mission fields of New Zealand, strong and full of energy. His board must be 12 feet long and is made of the most beautiful, laminated wood I have ever seen. It is polished to a shiny gloss and looks like a surfboard Duke Kahanamoku would gloat over. He tells me, "Your Dad taught me how to surf," and then calls out to me in his Māori tongue:

"Me haere ki te ngaru, Mike!"

Without thought, I somehow know he said, "Let's go surfing, Mike!"

Dad hands me the third surfboard, and I am aghast to see my Hobie Corky Carroll "Super Mini" model, which he bought me at the Hobie Surf Shop in San Clemente in 1968. *What?* It's as new as the day we picked it up, with the exact blue, yellow, and green acid splash color design. The bright colors radiate between the pure white foam. This thing would glow in the dark. Picking it up, I realize it is lighter than any surfboard I have ever held. I can't wait to catch my first wave on it. It is ready to go. I call back to them,

"Cowabunga dudes, let's go surfing!"

Surfing in Heaven? You *must* be kidding.

It is a dream come true.

Gazing out, I see a long strand of glittering ivory-white sand extending to the horizon with perfect waves rolling in like clockwork on both sides: right-facing waves on the left and left-facing waves on the right. I watch the waves on both sides in awe, mesmerized. Unbelievably clean barrels are peeling off in succession for as far as my eyes can see. Each wave is a flawless fusion of a point-break shoulder with a reef-break curl. I could not imagine a more ideal surfing spot. It is too good to be true. But we *are* in Heaven.

"Lefts or rights?" I call out to them as we pick up our boards. In saying that, I quickly realize we can go either way – there is no such thing as a goofy foot in Heaven. I laugh out loud.

Stepping into the water, I'm immediately struck by its pristine clarity as it washes over my legs. As I wade out, I see a bright, multicolored coral reef with a myriad of neon-colored fish amongst the rocks, as if I were peering into a vast aquarium. Pausing to take it all in, it hits me: I am really going surfing in Heaven.

The three of us are a picture of God's abundant provision as we radiate smiles of joy in anticipation of what is to come. "Yeehaw!" I call out as the first wave rolls over me with a sweet taste and aroma that rejuvenates my spirit as if washing away earthly worries. My body rinses completely dry like water off a duck's back. *Huh?* Paddling over my next wave, I am sprayed by a feathering lip that trails a spectacular rainbow of colors in its wake. Looking down, I notice I'm wearing my yellow "Hang Ten" surf trunks from my grammar school days in Corona del Mar. I chuckle, thinking how much I love them.

We quickly stroke around the breaking sections with Uncle Charles leading the way. I joke to Uncle Charles and Dad as we crest over yet another feathering rainbow-colored lip, "Only in Heaven would I let that one go by."

The white water explodes in brilliant white light as each wave breaks, as if light-emitting plankton illuminate the foam with the radiance of day. The contrast with the clear water is literally out of this world, like painting daylight onto a nocturnal night sky. I gasp at the beauty of it all before me and give the glory to God:

"His love endures forever."

As I paddle further out, the endless stretch of bleached white sand unfolds before me, waves breaking on the distant horizon as far as I can see. Only when I decide to sit up and rest on my board, taking a moment to absorb the breathtaking vista, does the interconnectedness of everything in Heaven truly dawn on me. God's intelligent design of it all blows my mind.

Beneath me is an extraordinary collection of colored, vibrant plants, darting fish, and rocks emitting light rays as bright as daylight. It resembles a Hawaiian coral reef, yet the intensity and vividness surpass anything I've ever witnessed. I am transfixed by the spectacle, unable to tear my gaze away. Dad and Charles share in my joy, their laughter echoing as they witness the sheer delight on my face.

Dad calls out, "The Earth was like a black-and-white movie, Michael."

Unable to resist the allure of the rejuvenating water, I plunge from my board into the depths of the water. Astonished, I can see perfectly and continue to breathe and talk underwater. "This is crazy!" I shout. Fish of unimaginable varieties and colors glide toward me as if they are a part of the homecoming celebration. I swim to the surface to tell Charles and Dad about my discovery.

They call back, "Welcome to Heaven, Mike."

Sitting on my board, the golden glory of the sky is powerful without any heat or potential for sunburn. Above, clouds of indescribable diversity streak across the stratosphere like a living canvas, painted with colors unfamiliar to my eyes. A profound sense of belonging washes over me as I acknowledge I am finally home. I lift my voice to praise God for it. Heaven is so much more than I imagined.

Time is lost but irrelevant. There are no boundaries around how long I have been out. The ocean and I are one. Amidst this vast expanse of beauty, I feel a profound sense of unity with the rhythms of the waves around me.

"His love endures forever."

I see Dad crossing a beautiful crystal blue breaking wave that is well overhead and feathering a rainbow of vivid colors behind him. He drags his foot off the tail of his Simmons Foam Sandwich to make a sweeping bottom turn and lets out a loud hoot as he sails by me, drawing a straight line across the face of the brilliantly clear water faster than I have ever seen him go. It is a sight to behold. My Dad is ripping across an eight-foot wall on a 1940s vintage balsa surfboard. I howl at him, "Woo-yah, Dad!" His bright smile is ear to ear as he attempts to take it all in.

A magnificent sight unfolds as I gaze behind him: seven pelicans soar in flawless unison, their pristine white feathers illuminated by golden-tipped wings, just skimming the lip of the approaching wave. I somehow know they are telling me, "This is *your* wave." Swiveling my board around in eager anticipation, I push off with just a single paddle and suddenly fly down the silky-smooth face of a double overhead wall of crystalline water shimmering in light from below. The pelicans gracefully swoop alongside, signaling the arrival of my moment to surf in Heaven.

I stand up and realize my balance is solid, and my feet are gripping my board as if with booties. There's no fear of falling. I howl praises to God.

"How great Thou art, Lord."

Screaming across the towering face of the wave feels like racing downhill from the top of a snow-covered mountain on skis. The brilliance of the underwater sea life lights my path as I lean right and carve a long, effortless bottom turn. My speed thrusts forward like the afterburners on a jet plane as I stare down the unusually thin lip of the wave ahead, knowing I will make it.

With unwavering confidence in my skills, I begin carving up and down the wave when, suddenly, seven pure white dolphins surge into the wave from behind me as if awaiting my presence. They cruise in formation, leading the way like an escort of military fighter jets. Their majestic presence fills me with awe as they effortlessly navigate the wave, their gaze locked onto me, anticipating my every move. The symmetry and elegance of their surfing prowess are beyond words. I follow them turn for turn as we glide along the strand, exchanging joy with each turn, lost in the perfect harmony of God's eternal creation. [3]

The wave transforms into a soft Steamer Lane-style shoulder as I jet out ahead of the break to carve a roundhouse cutback that makes a complete half-circle around the dolphins, back toward the curl. Like breadcrumbs on a path, my trail along the wave is marked in the brilliant white light of the foam as I crank each turn. As I race by their glimmering hulks, the dolphins launch into the air in perfect formation.

Launching a powerful floater off the crest of the white water, I smoothly transition back onto the building face of the wave as the dolphins shepherd me into the next section of the wave, propelling me forward with exhilarating momentum. The sand is glimmering in the shore break as I streak by faster than I have ever dreamed of going on a surfboard, catching a glimpse of Dad watching from the shack in his Coast Hardware beach chair. He smiles broadly as I consider how often he watched me surf over the years.

The Green Room

Then, in an instant, a breathtaking transformation unfolds around me. My world is suddenly bathed in a glorious shade of brilliant green as the double overhead curl engulfs me, seeming to close out the wave entirely. I center myself into the barrel of the wave, perfectly balanced as I ride inside a green tunnel toward a light brighter than the sun. As I hurtle forward, all traces of fear vanish, replaced by an overwhelming sense of purpose. It feels as though my physical and spiritual selves have merged seamlessly with the energy of this wave. Joy overwhelms me as I realize this is beyond anything I have ever experienced. It's as if I am in slow motion, almost floating, as the surge of the wave carries me deeper into a brilliant cloud of green spray drawing me to a radiant light. This light beckons me forward as I am humbled by the sight of God's everlasting love. Every atom of my being resonates with this divine connection. It is paradise. I have never felt better. Wave after wave of God's love washes through me. I realize, this is God. He is light. And His love is everlasting. Gratitude overflows as I offer thanks to God, my doubts swept away by the undeniable truth of this sacred moment. Words fail to capture the depth of my connection to the Creator of all things. Why did I doubt it? Words cannot do justice to this moment. Like Moses at the burning bush, I am on holy ground. [7]

"His love endures forever."

In that timeless moment, I felt a profound unity with God. Jesus is precisely who He claimed to be – a manifestation of pure love, the embodiment of the One True Light. In Him, there is no darkness at all. [8] Wave after wave of God's pure liquid light continues to wash through me as I soak in the promise of His unconditional love. Just one drop of it is enough to change the course of my life, yet I have oceans of it cleansing me of any questions I harbored about God's love.

Lost in the embrace of this sacred moment, I am next airborne, floating out of the green room as if I were ET riding his bicycle into the sunset. Behind me, the wave thunder claps with power as I land gracefully onto the shoulder, comforted by the gentle back spray of warm raindrops around me. An irrepressible grin stretches across my face, though I struggle to comprehend the magnitude of what just transpired. My soul is at peace. My joy is complete.

The Hodads will have to hear about this one. The green room is much more than I could imagine. I want to go back in, but the wave keeps me accelerating forward as the dolphins take one final jump in unison as they kick out from the back of the wave. As I try and reflect on the depth of God's love for me, I hear the praises of the angels singing from above:

"Angels, from the realms of glory,
Wing your flight o'er all the Earth;
Ye who sang creation's story,
Now proclaim Messiah's birth." [9]

Gliding across the shoulder onto open and flat water, just like a water skier slicing through the glassy waters of Lake Tahoe, I leave the breaking section of the wave behind at full speed as if I am preparing to kick out. Yet my momentum continues as I crank another turn on the serene open water. I see Mom watching from the shack with her patented Charlene smile, radiating the timeless charm of a Malibu beachgoer from the 1950s. With a final cut back on the flat water, I ride towards the shore for my kick out onto the warm sand as the cool, crystal-clear water carries me up onto the beach.

I feel more at home than ever before. All my worries, anxieties, and concerns are lost. Finally, I can rest. This is the life He planned for me. Heaven is where I belong. Hallelujah to our Lord of creation.

The reality of Heaven changes everything. I am overwhelmed with joy, gratitude, and love for a God who can provide such perfection. It's all about God's love. I pray the love God has waiting for *you* in Heaven may dramatically change your life *today*. Go and *shout* this truth to every surfer you know.

Let Heaven fill your thoughts; don't spend your time worrying about things down here.

— Colossians 3:23 (TLB)

Notes

1. Matthew 21:21 (NIV)

   "Jesus replied, "Truly I tell you, if you have faith and do not doubt, not only can you do what was done to the fig tree, but also you can say to this mountain, 'Go, throw yourself into the sea,' and it will be done."

2. John 14:2 (KJV)

   "In my Father's house are many mansions: if it were not so, I would have told you. I go to prepare a place for you."

3. Genesis 1:1 (NIV)

   "In the beginning God created the heavens and the earth."

4. Springer, Rebecca. Intra Muros: My Dream of Heaven. 1898.

5. Job 12:7-10 (NIV)

   "But ask the animals, and they will teach you,
    or the birds in the sky, and they will tell you;
   or speak to the Earth, and it will teach you,
   or let the fish in the sea inform you.
   Which of all these does not know
   that the hand of the Lord has done this?
   In His hand is the life of every creature
   and the breath of all mankind.

6. "Love endures forever." (Psalm 136, NIV)

   "His love endures forever." (Repeated 26 times in Psalm 136)

7. Exodus 3:1-5 (NIV)

    "Now Moses was tending the flock of Jethro his father-in-law, the priest of Midian, and he led the flock to the far side of the wilderness and came to Horeb, the mountain of God. There the angel of the Lord appeared to him in flames of fire from within a bush. Moses saw that though the bush was on fire, it did not burn up. So Moses thought, "I will go over and see this strange sight – why the bush does not burn up."

    "When the Lord saw that he had gone over to look, God called to him from within the bush, "Moses! Moses!"

    And Moses said, "Here I am."

    "Do not come any closer," God said. "Take off your sandals, for the place where you are standing is holy ground."

8. 1John 1:5-7 (NIV)

    "This is the message we have heard from him and declare to you: God is light; in him there is no darkness at all. If we claim to have fellowship with him and yet walk in the darkness, we lie and do not live out the truth. But if we walk in the light, as he is in the light, we have fellowship with one another, and the blood of Jesus, his Son, purifies us from all sin."

9. "Angels from the Realms of Glory" is a Christmas carol written by Scottish poet James Montgomery. It was first printed in the Sheffield Iris on Christmas Eve 1816

    Source:
    https://en.wikipedia.org/wiki/Angels_from_the_Realms_of_G lory

28. The End of the Story

Everyone wants to go to Heaven, but nobody wants to die.
— Joe Louis (Legendary American Boxer)

My good friend, Tom Klope, reads the last chapter of every book first. I was baffled when he first explained this, as I could not imagine wanting to know the ending of a book before you read it. Tom quickly pointed out that knowing how the book ended helped him enjoy it as he read. And if he didn't like how it ended, he might not read it.

For those of you who haven't yet read the Bible (Genesis to Revelation), I'm going to play Tom Klope and go right to the end of the story. No matter what, to truly grasp the significance of Heaven, you need to know how the Bible ends. I'll bait you to promise that the ending will include some intriguing evidence suggesting that surfing in Heaven is not so far-fetched.

Read that Book!

In April 1990, my wife Marla and I attended our first church service in Northern California at Peninsula Bible Church (PBC) in Palo Alto. We were newly married and had just relocated to northern California from Orange County. The church we attended in Newport Beach (Mariners Church) was modeled after PBC, so it was logical to give them our first visit in our search for our Sunday worship. I can remember feeling quite out of place, settling into an uncomfortable wooden pew at the very back of the church. A sense of unfamiliarity washed over us as we realized we did not recognize a single person.

The worship music seemed fine and a little bit familiar. Then, pastor Ray Stedman was introduced. Ray slowly stepped up to the podium, appearing as an older, stately gentleman wearing a sport coat and tie with a graying Butch Cassidy mustache framing his face. Neither Marla nor I knew a thing about Ray Stedman and his profound legacy as a pastor at PBC. What we did know was this entire scene looked quite different from what we had become familiar with in Newport Beach.

At Mariners Church, Pastor Kenton Bashore led the congregation with a youthful energy. Kenton sported a full head of blond hair, suntanned skin, and wore the casual dress you would expect in Newport Beach, as if the surfboards were on the car as soon as the service let out. Best of all, they had comfy cushioned chairs.

Only several months later did we discover we had attended Ray Stedman's final sermon after 40 years at PBC. One of the great pastors and leaders of our generation [1] was calling it quits on the day we showed up for a test drive at his church. He had retired and was moving with his wife to Oregon. Ray preached over 800 sermons and authored 28 books over those 40 years. His final message that day was on the final two chapters of the Bible (Revelation 21 & 22). I had *never* read Revelation. All I knew about Revelation was that it covered the end times when Jesus returns to Earth. [2]

I would like to tell you Ray's sermon was so remarkable I can remember specific details about what he said. In fact, I only remember three words. However, those words have stuck with me, like gorilla glue on wood, for over 30 years.

Toward the end of his sermon, Ray paused, held up his Bible at the pulpit, and called out to us (to *me*, it seemed), "Read that book!" Then, a couple of minutes later, he did it again, the Bible thudding on the pulpit: "READ THAT BOOK!"

His eyes seemed to look my way as if he were telling *me* to listen up. I assume everyone else felt the same way, but I never asked since we didn't know anyone.

I was convicted. I needed to *read that book.*

That was the first and only time Marla and I saw Ray Stedman preach. He was taken home to the Lord two and a half years after that sermon and just two days after his seventy-fifth birthday. "That Book" Ray referred to is the final book in the Holy Bible, Revelation. Ray's sermon that day was titled "The City of Glory." [3] It was all about Heaven. As it turns out, Heaven *is* the end of the story of the Bible. Yet, it is also the *beginning* of our eternal future with God. This incredible story of the Bible ends with the very best part – Heaven comes down to a renewed Earth, and eternity with God begins.

Thank you, Ray Stedman. I soon read that book.

Revelation

Even for a theologian, studying the book of Revelation can be like trying to solve a Rubik's Cube in the dark. It is a complex set of messages and symbolism for humankind to digest. I don't plan to go there. I am far from qualified.

I want to focus on the promise in the book of Revelation of a "lived happily ever after" ending in Heaven. That *is* the end of the story. Those who believe are *in Heaven with God for eternity.*

In the words of Ray Stedman, "It [the Book of Revelation] is indeed good news!"

Revelation aims to instill hope and reassurance in followers of Jesus Christ, assuring them of His imminent return. Often called the Revelation of Jesus Christ, the book centers around Him as the pivotal figure of both its narrative and all of history. Through its pages, the triumph over evil is depicted conclusively, with God offering the forever promise of an extraordinary future in Heaven for those who hold faith.

It is no accident that Revelation is the last of the 66 books of the Bible. The book gathers essential themes from the entire Bible and brings them into focus. It has a *lot* to say about Heaven. The concluding two chapters of Revelation (Revelation 21 & 22) end the Bible with amazingly descriptive details about Heaven. Revelation 21 describes how Jesus sets up his kingdom of Heaven on the New Earth and calls it the "New Jerusalem." In this New Jerusalem, believers will spend eternity with God in their resurrected bodies. In essence, Heaven returns to Earth with Jesus as our King in a world free of all sin.

I'd like to end this book by investigating one last question about Heaven. Could part of our experience on this renewed Earth include a little surfing? Revelation reveals four things about this New World to support the idea that surfing is very much in the realm of possibilities.

1 – Heaven will be a physical place.

Revelation describes this New World as a physical place with physical objects like trees, crops, rivers, houses, mountains, and more. It even describes us feasting on good food and well-aged wine. [4] According to the Bible, our resurrected Earth will be "like new." [5] The author of Revelation (the Apostle John) describes in detail a solid, physical world we will live in. From everything I know, it will be Heaven on Earth.

Before his death, Jesus told His disciples His Father's house had many rooms. [6] He promised to go and prepare a place for them and to return to take them there. I read this to say a designated home awaits us in Heaven. It sounds like a Master Architect customizes the construction to precisely what we would enjoy. I like the sound of that.

Even the Book of Isaiah (written hundreds of years before Christ) speaks of the creation of new Heavens and a new Earth so breathtaking no one will even think about the old Earth anymore. [7] My wife and I traveled to Israel in 2023, and one of the highlights of the trip was viewing the Dead Sea Scrolls, first discovered in 1947 after being in a cave near the Dead Sea for over two thousand years. One of those scrolls was the Book of Isaiah, which was nearly 100 percent preserved. It is hard to argue with that.

Case closed.

There does not seem to be much debate here – we will be in a physical world with physical objects doing physical things. I like how the late Roger Williams described it at a Mount Hermon Family camp on the shores of Lake Tahoe:

"If you think this is a beautiful place to live now – wait until you see it REDEEMED in Heaven!"

2 – We will be physical beings.

The Bible clearly states we will be reunited with our physical bodies in Heaven and walk the renewed Earth as physical beings. There are more Bible passages on this than I can track. One example is verse 5 of Revelation 21, which states, "I am making everything new." [8] God's rebirth of His physical creation also applies to the new resurrected bodies we will receive when Jesus returns.

The Bible describes how our heavenly bodies will be transformed, just like Jesus' resurrected body was when He appeared to the disciples following His death on the cross. [9] From all accounts, the physical appearance of Jesus *after* the resurrection was no different than *before* His death. [10] People recognized Him and felt His physical body to validate it was Him. He was not a ghost.

We also will be doing things we do today on Earth, like eating. There is a scene in the Gospel of John (John 21:1-14) where Jesus shows up on a beach in His resurrected body and cooks a fish breakfast over a charcoal fire with the disciples. [11] My wife and I visited that beach on our trip to Israel on the Sea of Galilee (called "The Place of the Coals"). As we stood on the beach at the water's edge, it was remarkable to visualize Jesus enjoying a meal with the disciples over a hot coal-burning fire. This scene shows us our bodies will be capable of eating and drinking and doing activities we do today, like having a BBQ on the beach with our friends.

What would stop us from paddling out for a few waves?

3 – There will be water.

The Book of Revelation speaks of a great river flowing through Heaven's main street. [4] This passage, among many others, assures us water will be abundant in Heaven. Surely, the river has a source and a destination that starts or ends in a large body of water. It seems reasonable to speculate the existence of large lakes like ours on Earth today. Remember, this is the Earth we live on today, in a renewed state. These lakes could very well act as freshwater oceans on the New Earth.

The Great Lakes region in North America contains over 20 percent of all the fresh water on planet Earth today. Because of that, a thriving community of surfers enjoy the shores of Lake Michigan. The movie *Step into Liquid* (by Dana Brown, son of famed filmmaker Bruce Brown) has a fun surfing scene showing these guys getting stoked catching waves on the shores of Sheboygan, Wisconsin, a thousand miles from the nearest ocean.

Who would say we could not have something even better on a renewed Earth? Again, I ask, if Kelly Slater (eleven-time world champion surfer) can create a near-perfect 6-foot barreling wave in a desert in California's Central Valley (kswaveco.com), could not our great God fulfill the promise of Heaven with something even better? I believe the room Jesus is preparing for me in Heaven could include waves *and* a surfboard. If you see that as far-fetched, read on to #4.

4 – We will be living with God.

Let's be clear: aside from Jesus, nobody on Earth has ever lived with God. [12] The book of Revelation ushers in a new era when the name "Immanuel" (God with us) will find its ultimate fulfillment. The prospect of living with the creator of the universe in Heaven tells me we are in for a few awe-inspiring surprises. Big time.

Remember, this is the God who created it *all* in the first place. This last book of the Bible fulfills God's commitment to dwell among His people. His grand plan of redemption for every one of us is accomplished. Imagine the infinite comfort and peace of living with God. This kind of living takes John Wooden's "Peace of Mind" to a whole new level. I believe once you place God into the picture of our home in Heaven, surfing becomes a slam dunk. (Pun intended, Mr. Wooden.)

God announces at the end of the Book of Revelation an emphatic, "I am making everything new!" Those one- to two-foot ankle biters Dana Brown filmed on the shores of Sheboygan, Wisconsin, could suddenly be transformed into the perfect waves his Dad filmed in *The Endless Summer* in 1966.

Why not?

Will There Be Seas in Heaven?

Revelation 21 contains a detailed description of what this "New Jerusalem" will look like, including this statement about the absence of a sea:

". . . .and there was no longer any sea on the new earth." (Revelation 21:1, NIV)

Throughout Scripture, the "sea" is symbolic of chaos and disorder, which will be absent in the New Jerusalem. Many Bible scholars believe this is the meaning of Revelation 21:1; the turbulence of our present age on Earth will no longer be present in the New Jerusalem. We will be at peace in Heaven.

Even if we assume this statement means that all saltwater seas are removed from the Earth in the New Jerusalem, it does not necessarily mean that all large bodies of water and beaches are gone.

In his book *Heaven*, Randy Alcorn makes an argument for having large bodies of water in Heaven:

"Another reason I believe the New Earth will have large bodies of water is that, as I argue in chapter 39, the same animals that inhabit our current planet will inhabit the New Earth. Most animal species live underwater, not on land, and most of those live in the ocean. (It would certainly be no problem for God to refashion such creatures to live in freshwater.)"

The End of the Story

The Bible tells the story of God creating the world as humanity's perfect home. [13] Then Satan entered the world to destroy that. [14] We see Satan gaining the upper hand daily in the news today. He wants to ensure we believe Heaven does not exist. [15] Sometimes, it seems like everything that could go wrong is going wrong in this world.

Yet the book of Revelation records the glorious ending where Jesus returns to defeat Satan and shepherd in the New Heaven and Earth. It will not be a mystical paradise. Revelation describes a solid, physical world of eternity that very well could have perfect waves to surf.

You now know the end of the story. I want to encourage you to "read that book!" After more than 30 years of studying the Bible, I am absolutely certain about God's plan for us to be in Heaven with Him when we die. One hundred percent.

Eternity is a real thing. Don't miss the chance to catch your perfect wave.

Your word is a lamp for my feet, a light on my path.
— Psalm 119:105 (NIV)

Notes

1. "Ray Stedman was one of the great pastors and leaders of a generation of evangelicals that is quickly passing away."

    raystedman.org/thematic-studies/ray-stedman/introduction

2. Revelation 1:7 (NIV)

    "Look, He is coming with the clouds," and "every eye will see Him, even those who pierced Him"; and all peoples on earth "will mourn because of Him." So shall it be! Amen."

    Revelation 22:6-7 (NIV)

    "The angel said to me, 'These words are trustworthy and true. The Lord, the God who inspires the prophets, sent His angel to show His servants the things that must soon take place.'"

    1 Thessalonians 4:16 (NIV)

    "For the Lord himself will come down from Heaven, with a loud command, with the voice of the archangel and with the trumpet call of God, and the dead in Christ will rise first."

3. "The City of Glory" sermon by Ray Stedman on April 29, 1990.

    Revelation 22:1 – 22:21

    https://www.raystedman.org/new-testament/revelation/the-city-of-glory

4. Revelation 22:1-2 (NIV)

    "And He showed me a pure river of water of life, clear as crystal, proceeding out of the throne of God and of the Lamb. In the midst of the street of it, and on either side of the river, was there the tree of life, which bare 12 manners of fruits, and yielded her fruit every month: and the leaves of the tree were for the healing of the nations."

Revelation 2:7 (NIV)

"Whoever has ears, let them hear what the Spirit says to the churches. To the One who is victorious, I will give the right to eat from the tree of life, which is in the paradise of God."

Isaiah 25:6 (NIV)

"Here on Mount Zion in Jerusalem, the Lord Almighty will spread a wondrous feast for everyone around the world – a delicious feast of good food, with clear, well-aged wine and choice beef."

5. Revelation 21:1-5 (NIV)

"Then I saw a New Heaven and a New Earth, for the first Heaven and the first Earth had passed away, and there was no longer any sea. I saw the Holy City, the New Jerusalem, coming down out of Heaven from God, prepared as a bride beautifully dressed for her husband. And I heard a loud voice from the throne saying, 'Look! God's dwelling place is now among the people, and He will dwell with them. They will be His people, and God himself will be with them and be their God. He will wipe every tear from their eyes. There will be no more death or mourning or crying or pain, for the old order of things has passed away.'

The former things will not be remembered, nor will they come to mind. But be glad and rejoice forever in what I create, for I will create Jerusalem to be a delight and its people a joy.

I will rejoice over Jerusalem and take delight in My people; the sound of weeping and of crying will be heard in it no more. Never again will there be in it an infant who lives but a few days, or an old man who does not live out his years; the one who dies at a hundred will be thought a mere child; the one who fails to reach a hundred will be considered accursed. They will build houses and dwell in them; they will plant vineyards and eat their fruit."

"He who was seated on the throne said, 'I am making everything new!' Then He said, 'Write this down, for these words are trustworthy and true.'"

6. John 14:2 (NIV)

   "My Father's house has many rooms; if that were not so, would I have told you that I am going there to prepare a place for you?"

7. Isaiah 65:17-21 (NIV)

   "See, I will create New Heavens and a New Earth.

   "The former things will not be remembered, nor will they come to mind.

   But be glad and rejoice forever in what I will create, for I will create Jerusalem to be a delight and its people a joy.

   "I will rejoice over Jerusalem and take delight in My people; the sound of weeping and of crying will be heard in it no more. Never again will there be in it an infant who lives but a few days, or an old man who does not live out his years; the one who dies at a hundred will be thought a mere child; the one who fails to reach a hundred will be considered accursed. They will build houses and dwell in them; they will plant vineyards and eat their fruit."

8. Revelation 21: 5 (NIV)

   "He who was seated on the throne said, 'I am making everything new!' Then he said, 'Write this down, for these words are trustworthy and true.'"

9. John 20:27 (NIV)

"Then he said to Thomas, 'Put your finger here; see my hands. Reach out your hand and put it into my side. Stop doubting and believe.'"

10. Luke 24:39 (NIV)

"Look at my hands and my feet. It is I myself! Touch me and see; a ghost does not have flesh and bones, as you see I have."

Philippians 3:20-21 (NIV)

"But our citizenship is in Heaven. And we eagerly await a Savior from there, the Lord Jesus Christ, who, by the power that enables Him to bring everything under His control, will transform our lowly bodies so that they will be like His glorious body."

11. John 21:10-14 (NIV)

"Jesus said to them, 'Bring some of the fish you have just caught.' So Simon Peter climbed back into the boat and dragged the net ashore. It was full of large fish, but even with so many the net was not torn. Jesus said to them, 'Come and have breakfast.' None of the disciples dared ask him, 'Who are you?' They knew it was the Lord. Jesus came, took the bread and gave it to them, and did the same with the fish. This was now the third time Jesus appeared to His disciples after He was raised from the dead."

12. John 3:13 (NIV)

"No one has ever gone into Heaven except the one who came from Heaven – the Son of Man."

13. Genesis 1:1 (NIV)

"In the beginning God created the Heavens and the Earth."

14. Genesis 3 (NIV)

"The fall of man."

15. John 8:44 (NIV)

"You belong to your father, the devil, and you want to carry out your father's desires. He was a murderer from the beginning, not holding to the truth, for there is no truth in him. When he lies, he speaks his native language, for he is a liar and the father of lies."

Acknowledgments

Creating this book was a collaborative effort involving many friends and family members who provided invaluable input over several years. While I can't mention everyone by name, I am deeply grateful to all who contributed. To those not specifically named, you know who you are – God bless you for your selfless support and generous heart. Your contributions have been instrumental in making *Surfing in Heaven* a reality.

First and foremost, my beautiful bride, Marla, has been at my side with this book for the past ten years, encouraging, editing, and, at times, loving this story as it came together. This book would never have left the launch pad without her faithful support. Marla, you have exemplified to me what marriage is all about. I love you.

Phil Nicholson, your honest insights were invaluable to the final edition of this book. Those unforgettable opening-day 49er games at Candlestick Park with our boys are locked into my memory for eternity.

Dennis Paoletti, I cherished our coffee meetings and your detailed analysis of each chapter. Thank you for taking such a genuine interest in this story. You were clearly my "Coach Wooden" throughout this amazing adventure.

Jack Schott, you have been by my side on this project from the very beginning. As the oldest Hodad of all (almost), you deserve special recognition. I still marvel at how you out-surfed us on that cold winter day in Monterey wearing a 6mm wetsuit with a serious flu bug. You are the man. Thank you, Jack, for everything, but most of all for your friendship.

To paraphrase author Anne Lamott, almost all good writing begins with a shitty first draft. My beta reading team pulled me out of the trenches from that awkward first draft (aka "Hodads!"). It *was* shitty. Lol. You all showed me there was a future for what I was writing, and for that, I am eternally grateful. Mike Benkert, John Davis, Craig Duncan, Nigel Endersby, Kim Herminghaus, Dr. Andrew Jones, Skip Lauderbaugh, Mark Ledwith, Mark Magiera, Reid Miller, John Park, and Pastor Danny Wallen – thank you for *all* of your feedback, support, pictures, and unsolicited encouragement. It's nice to know you're not the only one in the water. I look forward to surfing in Heaven with each one of you.

I had a team of editors over a few years who contributed to this book – each one of you was a piece of the puzzle that completed my story. Thank you to: Holly Crawshaw, Morgan Vandiver, Kim Autrey, and a special credit to Rachel Hills, who finally brought me home with a completed manuscript.

I would also like to acknowledge Katie Kelly's encouragement and support in my telling of Ben Kelly's story (Chapter 26: Kicking Out). Ben exemplified how to live life to the fullest here on Earth. God bless you, Katie.

A special thank you to my sister, Terry Hankenson, for helping me fill in so many blank spots in my memories of our idyllic days growing up at the beach in Corona del Mar. Those are some fond memories.

I must extend my heartfelt thanks to Thomas Umstattd and his Author Media community. When I decided to self-publish this book, I had no idea what I was doing. Thomas's team and online resources were my saving grace through this entire process.

Pastor René Schlaepfer, you deserve the credit for setting me on this path back in 2004 at the Mount Hermon family camp on Lake Tahoe. God bless you.

Thank you, God, for planting this story on my heart as I listened to René describe the wonders of Heaven that await us.

Finally, I wish to acknowledge the spiritual guidance over many years of my Bible Study Fellowship (BSF) Saturday morning men's leadership team. That time on our knees in prayer on Saturday mornings was as close as I could get to God on this side of Heaven. God bless you guys for demonstrating to me what faith is all about. This book is a direct outcome of your many prayers.

Appendices

I. Author's Notes

1. The Bible is a massively complex story. As a surfer who started this journey in my thirties without any formal training in the Bible, it took me years of studying to begin to piece together the 66 books and nearly 1,200 chapters that make up the Bible. The journey for me is far from over. There is so much more to learn. Without a formal Bible study, church group, or an organization like Bible Study Fellowship (BSF), it is a significant challenge to assimilate the story God has written. I was very fortunate to have excellent mentoring and leadership which has inspired me to pass that on. Please reach out to me at www.SurfingForBalance.com ("contact Mike") if you would like assistance with moving forward in your education.

2. The process of writing *Surfing in Heaven* has been transformational for me. As I look back on the journey, I am struck by wonder at how it all happened. God Himself placed this book on my heart. I know I am in God's will when this story has been so easy and joyful to write. It is a glorious feeling to experience the work of the Holy Spirit. I believe God has used my surfing background to enable me to reach out to surfers who don't yet know the end of the story. If just one of them shows up to paddle out with me in Heaven, this book will be an all-time best-seller. To refuse to embrace Jesus as God's Son is to lose the greatest gift of love ever offered in the history of mankind.

3. Ink drawings for this book are by artist Scott Sutton, a native Californian born in Santa Monica in 1952. Scott has authored and illustrated 17 popular children's books, including the treasured "*Family of Ree*" series of books. He shares a special bond with author Mike Mulkey, carving out unforgettable memories surfing in southern California in the 1960s. Scott's artistic journey began in Junior High School in 1966 when his first cartoon found its

way into the pages of Surfer Magazine. That cartoon (pictured below) gave Scott instant fame among our CdM surfing community, as well as setting the stage for his remarkable career as an artist and storyteller. More on Scott can be found at scottesutton.com.

II. About the Author

Mike Mulkey is a surfer, author, and life coach who writes about finding the perfect wave in Heaven. His passion for helping people tackle work-life balance led him to launch "SurfingForBalance.com" in 2014 to blog about his struggles to stay afloat amidst the chaos in Silicon Valley. Mike is now living out his dream of working part-time at Trader Joe's and writing about hanging ten toes over the nose.

More on Mike can be found at:
SurfingForBalance.com/presskit

Thank you for reading my book! I would greatly appreciate it if you could take 5 minutes to leave a review on Amazon. Instructions at:
SurfingForBalance.com/resources

III. Circle of Life Quiz

If we don't change the direction we are going, we are likely to end up where we are headed.

— Ancient Chinese Proverb

The "Circle of Life Quiz" is a personal development tool designed to visually assess the balance in your life. It divides life into three essential areas for evaluation: work, family, and self.

This tool aims to ensure you evenly allocate your time and energy across all aspects of your life. The primary goal of the tool is to foster improvement in your professional life, enhance your family life, and support your personal well-being, creating a harmonious balance among work, family, and self.

Let's get started – you can download a PDF of the tool here:
  SurfingForBalance.com/resources

IV. Prayer to Receive Jesus Christ as Your Savior

Have you received Jesus Christ as your Savior from sin and as Lord of your life? If you have not, would you pray right now? You can pray aloud to Him with words from your heart, or you might want to pray this prayer:

> Father, I have sinned. I have not obeyed your Word. I have tried to run my own life. I have ignored You and Your will for me. I have tried to decide for myself what is right and wrong. I am lost unless You save me. Thank you for sending Your Son, the Lord Jesus Christ, to pay for my sin and guilt. Thank You for raising Him from the dead and giving Him authority over my life. I receive Him

as my Savior and Lord. I receive Your gift of eternal life
in Christ. I will turn from my sinful life to serve You. You
are my Creator and Redeemer.

Continue your prayer by telling God what you are thinking and
feeling.

V. "Going to Heaven" Booklist

Surfing in Heaven is a story about the unquenchable thirst God placed on
my heart for knowledge about what awaits us in Heaven. Writing this
book led me on a quest for resources that transcended our conventional
interpretation of Heaven. While the Bible remains our ultimate guide to
Heaven, this curated booklist (my "Top 10") offers perspectives
frequently overlooked in mainstream Christian circles.

You can download a PDF of the booklist here:
SurfingForBalance.com/resources

Surfing in Heaven Glossary

Out of the water, I am nothing.
— Duke Kahanamoku (Hawaiian swimmer and surfer)

Ankle Biter

- **Ankle Biter:** waves that are too small to surf seriously (unless a contest is going on…)
- **Back Spray:** ocean spray that hits you from behind when coming out of a tube ride
- **Balance**: the first thing you need to learn in surfing
- **Barrel**: the hollow interior of a breaking wave; tube
- **Bomb**: a massive wave
- **Bottom turn:** a turn made at the bottom of the wave
- **Bro**: fellow surfer (your brother or mate)
- **Corn dogging**: rolling your wet body in the warm sand so it sticks to you like a corn dog
- **Curl**: the breaking section of the wave
- **Cutback**: switching directions on the wave from the shoulder back toward the curl
- **Ding**: damage to the surface of your surfboard (usually a crack, hole, or fracture)

- **Drop-In:** the initial entry down the face of the wave (after paddling has stopped)
- **Duck dive:** pushing your surfboard under an incoming wave when paddling out
- **Eggbeater:** rotating your legs in a circular motion while sitting to position yourself for an incoming wave
- **Eight feet**: An eight-foot-high wave, measuring the height from the crest to the trough
- **Face**: the front of the wave before it has broken
- **Floater**: riding over the whitewater of a wave back onto the shoulder while turning the board as you float
- **Foam**: the section of the wave that has broken (whitewater, soup)
- **Foamers/Foaming**: the 1960s Corona del Mar term for waves breaking off the end of the jetty
- **Glassy:** no wind to ripple the face of the waves
- **Gnarly:** when the waves are heavy, intense, and difficult; it can be dangerous to surf
- **Goofy foot**: a surfer who rides waves with his right foot forward
- **Green Room:** the inside of a barrel or tube
- **Grom**: a kid surfer (grommet)
- **Half-pipe:** A snow-covered sloping channel at any ski resort with a U-shaped cross-section to allow skiers and snowboarders to perform aerials
- **Hanafin Bananafin**: Pat Hanafin had a surf shop in Newport Beach in the 1970s where he made his patented "Hanafin Bananafin" longboard
- **Hang Five**: five toes over the tip of the nose while riding a wave
- **Hang Ten**: ten toes over the tip of the nose while riding a wave; surf trunks brand from my grammar school days in Corona del Mar
- **Hanging 11**: when a male surfer rides his board in the nude

- **Hodad:** a non-surfing beach bum (a wannabe surfer)
- **Impact Zone:** the general area where waves are consistently breaking
- **Indicators**: a sheltered point right-hand break in Santa Cruz, California, part of Steamer Lane
- **Interval:** the time in seconds between waves
- **Kick out:** finishing a ride by turning back out over the top or shoulder of the wave you were on
- **Kook:** a rookie surfer who is clueless about surfing culture and protocol
- **Leash:** the polyurethane cord attached between your leg and your surfboard
- **Lefts**: a wave that breaks to the left for a surfer facing the shore
- **Lip:** the uppermost part of the wave just before it breaks
- **Longboard**: a long surfboard; generally, over nine feet long (with a rounded nose)
- **Lineup:** the area just beyond the breaking waves where surfers cluster to catch waves
- **Lull:** the time between sets of waves when the ocean is calm
- **Mavericks:** the famous big wave surf spot in Half Moon Bay, California
- **Maytagged:** getting tumbled by a large wave ("Maytag" brand of clothes washers)
- **Middlepeak**: a reef break in Santa Cruz, California, part of Steamer Lane
- **Nirvana:** surfing in Heaven (paradise)
- **Nose**: the very front of the surfboard
- **Overhead:** when the wave height is higher than your head
- **Peak**: the highest point of an approaching wave before it breaks
- **Pearling**: when a surfer's weight is too far forward, and the surfboard nose dives underwater (as if diving for pearls)

- **Point**: Pleasure Point in Santa Cruz, California, which is generally considered the stairs at 36th Avenue
- **Point Break**: waves that wrap around a point of landing, making for longer rides surfing
- **Power section**: the part of a wave closest to where it is breaking; often called the pocket
- **Quiver**: a surfer's collection of surfboards
- **Rails**: the sides of a surfboard, running from nose to tail
- **Reef Break**: waves that break over a rock or coral reef
- **Rights**: a wave that breaks to the right for a surfer facing the shore
- **Regular foot:** a surfer who rides waves with his left foot forward
- **Roundhouse:** a cut-back that continues around through an arc of 180 degrees back into the breaking section of the wave
- **Session:** the event of surfing; from when you paddle out until you come in
- **Set:** a group of waves that are approaching the beach together
- **Shore break:** mostly not surfable waves that break right on the shore
- **Shortboard:** a short surfboard; generally, less than seven feet long
- **Shoulder**: the part of the unbroken wave away from the curl
- **Slot**: a right-hand point break just inches from the cliff face in Santa Cruz, California, part of Steamer Lane
- **Stoked**: pumped, super happy, excited
- **Swell**: unbroken waves out at sea, often referred to by direction (e.g., south swell)
- **Tail**: the very back of the surfboard
- **Take-off:** the critical moment where a surfer commits to catching a wave
- **Tube**: the hollow interior of a breaking wave; barrel
- **Turtle**: a technique used by longboarders where they roll their board over to navigate through broken waves

- **Walk the nose**: the act of walking to the front/tip of the surfboard to nose-ride
- **Wall**: the face of the wave that is steep and not yet breaking
- **Wax**: what surfers rub onto the deck of their surfboard to improve traction
- **Whitewater:** the wave after it breaks (foam, soup)

Thank you to my Kickstarter Backers:

Aaron Olson, Alan Lu, Angela Carducci, Author Media, Brian Clemence, Bill Gough, Bill Purcell, Brian Cilker, Brian Wo, Bruce Barry, Chris Higgins, Chris Vargas, Craig & Jen Thompson, Craig Duncan, Dino Piscione, Doug Atler, Drew Jones, Jack Schott, Jeff Jones, Jennifer Hohmann, Jiajia Li, Joel Brown, John Arledge, John Lunsford, John Park, Jeff McMeekin, Karen J, Kelly Strenge, Kirtee Raparia, Kjersti Nelson, KT Park, Louis Dietz, Lynn Rohrer, Margaret Esther, Margaret Watts Romney, Mark Ledwith, Mark Magiera, Mark O'Dell, Melissa Marie, Mike Benkert, Norman Happ, Phil Nicholson, Rich Maher, Rick Kirschenbaum, Rob Luenberger, Robert Schlossman, Robert Hankenson, Robert McFarland, Scott Segelke, Scott Wharton, Tess Reynolds, Tom Musgrave, Venus Fung, William Viergever, William W. King

Visit Mike Mulkey at:

SurfingForBalance.com